# THE PHARAOHS
# MASTER-BUILDERS

**Egyptian architecture reaches perfection.**

The great hypostyle hall of the Temple of Horus at Edfu was built during the reign of Ptolemy VIII (c. 145 BC). The roof slabs are 50ft (15m) above the ground. On the right in the shadows lies a second hypostyle hall preceding the dark inner sanctum.

# THE PHARAOHS MASTER-BUILDERS

TEXT BY HENRI STIERLIN

PHOTOGRAPHS BY ANNE AND HENRI STIERLIN

TERRAIL

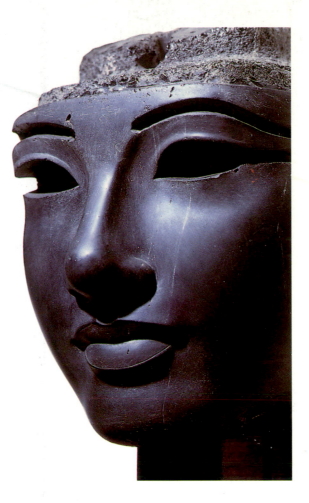

**The delicate, almost feminine face of the great builder, Amenophis III.**

The eyes and eyebrows formerly embedded with colored stones and the finely traced lips of this graceful portrait carved in obsidian have inspired much comment. Among the many creations of King Amenophis III are the temples of Amun in Karnak and Luxor, the Colossi of Memnon, the Amenophium (since destroyed) and his vast tomb in the Valley of the Kings.

Cover Illustration:

**The Temple of Horus at Edfu**

A colonnade built during the Ptolemiac period c. 116 BC.

Editors: Jean-Claude Dubost and Jean-François Gonthier
Art director: Bernard Girodroux
English adaptation: Frances Wister Faure
Composition & Filmsetting: Compo Rive Gauche, Paris

© FINEST S.A./ÉDITIONS PIERRE TERRAIL, PARIS 1992
© 1995 for the English edition
ISBN: 2-87939-020-6
Printed in Italy

**Stairs leading back down from the roof of the Temple of Horus at Edfu.**

A procession of priests descended this staircase from the Chapel of Irradiation where the sacred statues of the gods were presented to the rays of the sun. This section of the sanctuary erected under the Ptolemies dates from the 3rd century BC.

# CONTENTS

# INTRODUCTION

*Villages of the Nile Delta*
*hidden among the palm groves*
*and tilled plots of land.*

In ancient Egypt, pharaonic architecture evolved over a period of three thousand years. It took form as early as the Neolithic Age (6000-4000 BC), becoming widely established toward 3000 BC, continued to evolve in spite of a marked standstill during the reign of the Ptolemies, and came abruptly to an end during the Roman Empire in the 3rd century AD.

The Egyptians' primordial quest for eternal life led them to develop a lasting funerary architecture to commemorate their deceased sovereigns and their gods. For these monuments, the master-builders of the Nile Valley, abandoning the wattle-and-daub technique (mud walls made of woven reeds and trunks of palm trees and covered with a thatched roof) which, until recently, was still the principal

Opposite:

**Typical landscape of Upper Egypt: Aswan and Elephantine Island.**

The Valley of the Nile comes to its narrowest point at the Tropic of Cancer. This was Egypt's "southern gate" and was marked by a granite barrier at the first cataract. Luxuriant gardens were planted between the river and the desert. On the west bank is a rock-hewn necropolis where the tombs of the princes of Aswan who reigned at the end of the Old Kingdom were laid to rest. (c. 2200 BC).

9

mode of construction of domestic buildings along the Nile Valley from the Delta to Nubia. They transformed these primitive methods into a mudbrick technique that soon evolved into stonework. This process of *petrifaction* met their desire for enduring monuments and led to the construction of edifices which served emblematic functions, both ritualistic and mortuary.

The great historical structures which succeeded the mudbrick buildings of the Predynastic Period were essentially temples and tombs. The master-builders raised prodigious creations such as Cities of the Dead in the desert along the edge of the fertile valley, colossal pyramids in whose depth the kings of the Old Kingdom were laid to sleep for eternity, grandiose temples devoted to the gods and the cult of the sovereign, and royal hypogea with mazes deeply hewn into the western hills above Thebes.

Some of the great temples are so well preserved that we can still detect the architect's slightest intentions. In several sanctuaries from the New Kingdom and Ptolemaic Periods, the walls and the ceilings are intact, enabling us to appreciate the articulation of space and the flow through the different parts of the building. The roof slabs, still in place, let us admire the play of light on the polychrome wall paintings in the increasingly darker halls leading from the sun-baked courtyard to the shadowy inner sanctum, where a mysterious intimacy still reigns.

Temples, shrines, pyramids, tombs, rock-hewn sanctuaries, sacred lakes, and alleys of sphinxes take on another dimension when considered in connection with the ceremonies for which they were built. Many of the reliefs and wall paintings adorning these monuments contain holy formulas. Some show figures of priests reciting hymns while performing their duties, and sacred texts in hieroglyph explain the rituals at the exact spot where they took place. Others depict grandiose processions through echoing halls, pilgrimages by boat on the river, solemn funerary services in the Valley of the Kings, or military campaigns. Like annotations in a book, they throw light upon the builder's motives and explain the religious and political functions of the buildings, going far beyond our modern functionalism.

It is difficult for us to fathom this architecture of the past until we recognize its refusal of anything transient or ephemeral and its pledge of eternity to a civilization confronted by the desert and death. Studying the architecture of Ancient Egypt cannot be reduced to an

aesthetic approach or to an analysis based on technical or typological considerations; nor can the functional aspects be separated from the spiritual imperatives that ensured the permanence of traditional forms in Egyptian art. Because of the religious beliefs of their ancient civilization, the master-builders called millions of laborers to the pharaonic building sites and they united their efforts in order to perpetuate their faith in the Afterlife and in the power of their god-king.

## A Cosmology shaped by Nature

In order to understand Egyptian society, culture and art, and the rationale for its architecture, it is necessary first to take the natural surroundings into account. The Nile governs a narrow region full of life that blossoms in the heart of the most arid desert on Earth. It is an umbilical cord carrying its life-bringing flow over thousands of miles through the otherwise desolate hills, dunes and wastes that border it. Understandingly, this land had been referred to since Antiquity as the "Gift of the Nile." Although this cliché has become trite, it perfectly expresses the vital relationship between a natural environment, both hostile and favorable, and the spread of a civilization.

Seen on a map, the Nile takes the form of a huge flower with a stem reaching downward into tropical Africa and growing towards the more temperate zones of the north where it blooms into a large Delta. There, with its multiple branches, the river irrigates large surfaces of fertile soil formed by black silt from the floods, before turning into an immense delta with multiple branches and emptying into the Mediterranean Sea.

The formidable mass of water flowing from the great lakes of the rain forests and from the mountains of Abyssinia runs due north, while the sun above crosses the sky from the east to the west in its daily course. Both of these courses—the south/north flow of water and the east/west movement of the sun—played a major role in ancient Egyptian cosmology and gave rise to a dualistic concept of the cosmos with a highly-structured framework and systematic relationships.

The prevailing wind that blows up the valley in the opposite direction from the flow of the river provided remarkable tailwind for the many sailboats that have navigated there even since well before the first dynastic period. For northbound travel, the current sufficed to carry

Opposite:

**Life in an Egyptian house at the time of the New Kingdom.**

This tomb painting, copied in about 1820 by Ippolito Rosellini, depicts a house and its garden of trellises and ornamental trees. Women and children bring foodstuffs to be placed in a storeroom forming a vestibule (on the left). Servants are preparing libation tables. The dwelling itself is composed of a high ceiling supported by fine columns with open-papyrus capitals. The doors are surmounted by a classic Egyptian cavetto cornice.

**Two boats with multicolored square sails navigating on the Nile.**

A great stern oar was used to till the boat when under sail. The cabin on the deck housed passengers. This print by Rosellini was published in 1832.

the boats, but oars could be used for additional speed. For the return journey the boatmen raised a mast and yard, and hoisted a square sail enabling them to sail upstream effortlessly and to travel great distances southward above the first cataracts.

An entire civilization was able to construct a coherent spiritual vision, thanks to such a rich gift from nature. Sun, water and wind, along with the fertile alluvial soil of a seasonally flooded river-bed, constituted a complete, unified ecosystem. For the ancient Egyptians these natural constants formed the cosmological inventory from which their preoccupation with eternity and space would be elaborated.

## Worn by the passage of time and of men

Three thousand years of Pharaonic civilization have left us a legacy of truly remarkable creations that continue to stimulate the curiosity and admiration of an increasingly numerous public which undertakes "cultural pilgrimages" to discover these marvels of the past: colossal constructions, hauntingly beautiful sculptures, skillfully-crafted objects and superb wall paintings. Already in the time of Plato, a marked infatuation with the land of the pharaohs already inspired a vogue of Egyptomania, and expeditions to their monuments came to be considered indispensable by Hellenic and Roman philosophers and scientists. Since the end of the 18th century in the wake of Napoleon Bonaparte's military and scientific campaign, the Nile Valley once again became a focus of fascination, drawing millions of sightseers who gaze upon the Karnak columns, wander through the hypogea of the Valley of the Kings, and penetrate into the heart of the great pyramids of Giza.

The price of success, however, has been equally high and dramatic. The flow of tourists in the last fifty years in the tombs and temples, as well as the construction of the first dam on the Nile at Aswan, had such disastrous effects that certain masterpieces have been permanently lost. The royal tombs were not only plundered in the past, but their wall paintings, still brightly colored at the time of Champollion in 1820, have become oxidized by pollution. Carbon dioxide exhaled by the crowds in the confined spaces of small rooms, some hewn 330ft (100m) into the rock, have turned the colors into lusterless shades of gray.

This becomes painfully evident in a comparison between a watercolor copied in the early 19th century attesting to the freshness of the hues after three thousand years and the pitiful state revealed by a photograph taken recently in the same royal tomb in the Valley of the Kings. This illustration shows a wall painting in the tomb of King Sethos I such as it appeared at the time of Belzoni (1778-1823).

The temple of Isis at Philae, which was submerged for dozens of years under a lake formed by the old Aswan dam before being moved to another site, has lost all of the polychromy still present two centuries ago on its walls, ceiling and columns, as documented in *Description de l'Egypte* (1809). Furthermore, the opening of the Great Temple of King Ramesses II, after it was dug out of the sand in the 19th century, allowed moist air from the river to penetrate into the rock-hewn halls, causing irreparable damage. We can only regret the loss of the monument's bright colors that still existed when the teams of Italian Egyptologists headed by Ippolito Rosellini made the admirable copies which were published in Pisa in 1832. In order to give an idea of the warm and colorful appearance of the pharaonic buildings, we have to resort to the drawings made some two hundred years ago.

Such discouraging thoughts however should not dishearten those who wish to understand the artistic legacy of Egypt. All other forms of pictorial expression in the pharaonic world were subordinate to architecture. The admirable vestiges still to be seen in the Nile Valley prove that this civilization not only created and achieved the most formidable ensemble of constructions in history, but that it endowed them with a religious significance which is further demonstrated by the beauty of the reliefs, the perfection of the statuary, and the splendor of the paintings.

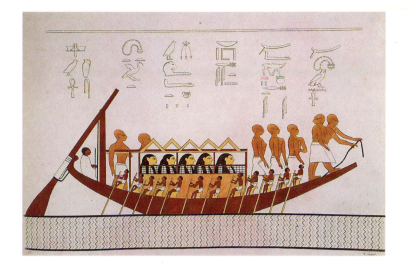

**Boat with twenty-four rowers and crew.**

A crew of seven men and a helmsman made the maneuvers; the privileged passengers traveling from one city to another sat in an airy yet covered cabin. Also a print by Rosellini executed after a tomb painting.

*Note: the reader will find an index-glossary of principal names and architectural terms used in archeology and Egyptology at the end of this book (pages 218-220).*

**Sacred cow with horns in the form of a lyre.**

This watercolor was painted by H. Salt in 1818 in the depths of the tomb
of King Sethos I (c. 1312-1301 BC) at the Valley of the Kings.
This panel, still high in color one hundred and seventy years ago,
decorated a small room situated to the right of the sarcophagus chamber.
The goddess Nut, representing starry skies, allows the barques of the
gods to pass under her belly. This refers to the course of the Sun,
according to ancient Egyptian cosmology.

**The same scene from King Sethos I's tomb in its disastrous state today.**

A comparison between the watercolor and this recent photograph shows the damage that the passage of millions of visitors have caused to this hypogeum hewn out of rock at a depth of a hundred meters under the mountain. Almost all the brilliant colors as attested by Belzoni, Rosellini, Champollion, and Mariette in the 19th century have disappeared forever.

# From Mudbrick to Quarried Stone

## THE MONUMENTS OF
## KING DJOSER AT SAQQARA

*The first Egyptian architecture: the girdle wall
enclosing King Djoser's necropolis; the perimeter
of the wall is more than a mile long.*

To a great extent Egypt's history was determined by natural environment. Topographic features and climatic changes greatly affected human settlements in the Nile Valley. The earliest inhabitants of this region emerged from a culture that was shaped during the Upper Paleolithic Age and gradually gave up the nomadic existence of a hunter-gatherer for the more sedate life of a Neolithic cultivator.

Ten or fifteen thousand years ago the geography of North Africa differed profoundly from what it is today. The area was covered by many verdant valleys and immense oases amid grassy steppes before a great change occurred that turned it into a wasteland. Wildlife was plentiful and plantlife abundant. The human population, scattered over a vast expanse of land roamed freely in

Opposite:

**The entrance to King Djoser's funerary monuments at Saqqara.**

This bastion which emerges from the girdle wall was built by the architect Imhotep (Third Dynasty, c. 2680 BC). It was brilliantly reconstructed in recent years using mostly the original stone blocks. The pilaster strips (*lesenes*) were transposed from the mudbrick structures of Predynastic Egypt. This system of construction with alternating recesses and salient angles was based on geometrical regularity and subsequently governed all Pharaonic architecture.

19

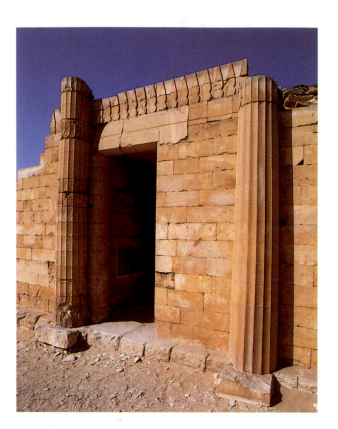

**The House of the South, part of King Djoser's complex at Saqqara.**

The fluted columns engaged in the wall of the façade appear as forerunners of the Doric style, twenty-two centuries before their time. The rigorous reconstruction (*anastylosis*) was performed by the French archeologist, Jean-Philippe Lauer. Inside, the space is very small and houses only a dummy room, more of a niche.

Opposite:

**The majestic portico of King Djoser's funerary complex at Saqqara.**

Preceding the south courtyard in front of the Step Pyramid, fasciculated columns resting directly on plinthsare embedded in the ends of walls and are topped by square abaci. From the start, Imhotep's stone architecture displays exceptional strength and purity of line.

pursuit of elephants, rhinoceroses, buffaloes and various wild animals which offered a plentiful supply of food. But a prolonged period of drought scorched the earth progressively and turned the land into deserts, existinguishing many species. Then a millennia-old lifestyle, much different from that of North Africa today, was profoundly and dramatically transformed.

Gradually, the fertile strip of the Nile offered the only possible refuge. There, the river accomplished miracles for it never dried out! A great variety of peoples drifting from both the East and West congregated on the steep banks of the river despite its impetuous floods and shifting marshlands.

The game that abounded in the thickets of rushes and reeds of the marshes around the Nile provided food for a time, but soon could not satisfy the needs of a growing population. This situation compelled the inhabitants of the region to change their habits. Gatherers turned into peasants and hunters into cattlemen, in a slow process that took place along the Nile Valley during the Ninth Millennium BC (Natufian Period).

In prehistoric times, more and more people settled in what was to become Egypt. Early monuments and the first hieroglyphs bear witness to an intense cultural activity. Each tribe brought with it its own gods, rituals and patterns of worship. During most of the 5th and 4th centuries BC, gradual transformation took place, producing a synthesis of ancient beliefs and a syncretism of the different religious systems and creating a common cosmogony and theology. A hierarchical pantheon was organized around triads of deities such as Horus, the father, Hathor, the mother, and Harsomtus, the son. This process of unification developed under the guidance of a powerful caste of priests.

In the meantime, local conflicts and tribal wars afflicted the Nile Valley and Delta giving ambitious overlords the opportunity to extend their domination over large regions. Eventually, two independent kingdoms were founded: Buto in the North and Nekhen in the South. The first kings nursed persistent ambitions to fuse these two Lands, for they were acutely aware of the fundamental unity of a territory that shared the wealth distributed by a generous river.

This long-sought-after unification process took place at the very end of the Fourth Millennium BC, when Upper and Lower Egypt—the Valley and the Delta—came under the rule of a single sovereign, the pharaoh, who wore the Double Crown, called the *pschent*, a combination of the miter-like

Three columns with capitals shaped like bunches of papyrus leaves are engaged in the wall of the House of the North in the Step Pyramid complex at Saqqara.

The designs created for King Djoser seem amazing to the modern eye. Such elegance is unexpected in structures built so long ago. The modern reconstruction demonstrates that Egyptian builders were able to conceive a consistent architectural language already around 2680 BC. The perfectly-shaped capitals are supported by engaged columns; each shaft artfully displays a stem-like ridge, a formal element that would later disappear from the Pharaonic repertory.

**The Jubilee Court in King Djoser's complex at Saqqara.**

The Hed-Sed festival, a ceremony designed to rejuvenate the powers of the pharaoh after a reign of thirty years, required a ritualistic complex. Shrines with cambered roofs surrounded a course that the king paced out when he took possession of his kingdom; the ceremony was repeated on his thirtieth jubilee. This five-thousand-year-old architecture has been painstakingly rebuilt with the original blocks.

Opposite:

**One of the shrines around the Jubilee Court in the complex built by Imhotep at Saqqara.**

The cambered roof, a reminder of traditional structures, rests on three thin fluted columns engaged in the wall with curious capitals in the form of leaf-like pendants. The masonry of this ceremonial architecture was made of small limestone blocks that were accurately squared and gave off a golden color in the sunlight. There is almost no empty space inside for rooms, for a solid rubble core lies behind the façades.

White Crown *(hedjet)* of Upper Egypt and the Red Crown of Lower Egypt *(deshret)*. The personality of the first ruler of the new state is clothed in mystery because of an almost total absence of written evidence, although the legendary King Menes is reputed to have ensured the first reunion of the Two Lands and founded a new city of White Walls, later called Memphis.

### The rhythm of history

If we are to understand the next thirty centuries of pharaonic architecture, we must bear in mind the fact that the Egyptian civilization was the longest lasting one of its kind. Even so, cultural development over such a long period of time was not a continuous process.

Modern historians divide the chronology of Egyptian history into three main periods: the Old Kingdom, the Middle Kingdom and the New Kingdom. Each of these periods followed a general cycle of birth, apogee, decline and re-birth, and were separated by obscure interludes, called the First and the Second Intermediate Periods.

The end of the New Kingdom (*c.* 1100 BC) did not imply the disappearance of Egyptian culture however, for Egypt remained a major political power. Many masterpieces were created during the First Millennium BC in the Tanite Period, during the Saite Renaissance (*c.* 664-525 BC), and under the Ptolemies (*c.* 305-30 BC). The construction of large temples continued throughout a Hellenistic Dynasty which ruled over Egypt from its capital city at Alexandria, and after Imperial troops annexed the region to Rome. Egyptian civilization underwent an irreversible process of disintegration when it could not resist the rise of Christianity; only then (*c.* AD 470) were its construction sites and workshops deserted.

Geography was a decisive factor in Egyptian history. The area had become a crossroads between the Near East and the Mediterranean world–between Asia and Africa–and occupied a naturally fortified position surrounded by deserts to the East and West. The inhabitants of Egypt could sally forth beyond their borders more easily than enemies could encroach on them. At a very early stage, Egyptians set up their rule over Palestine and Lebanon in order to obtain cedarwood for carpentry and shipbuilding, as well as over Nubia, beyond the First Cataract up the Nile River, to ensure a supply of myrrh and incense trees.

At its zenith, Egypt spread from the banks of the Euphrates in Syria to the Upper Nile at Napata, in Nubia, its kings launched expeditions as far as the Land of Punt.

### King Djoser's complex at Saqqara

Detail showing the wall in the south court with a frieze of cobras.
The flame-spitting snake protected the king from evil. Placed on the
pharaoh's forehead, the royal cobra (*uraeus*) was literally supposed to
scare the life out of his enemies.
Above. The first pyramid ever built in Egypt stands inside King Djoser's
sacred compound. It originated from step-shaped mastabas and displays
a still imperfect pyramidal shape. The structure rises to 200ft (70m)
above ground level.
Opposite. The column of the "T" Temple stood against King Djoser's Step
Pyramid dominating the Saqqara skyline. The ritual function of this
building is not clear. A frieze carved in lighter-colored stone displayed the
djed-pillar motif—a stylized representation of a leafless tree—symbolically
referring to the monarchy's hoped-for stability. In the left foreground, an
upright torus reinforces the junction of two surfaces of stonework.

**Two roughhewn statues in Djoser's complex.**

These statues are a deeply moving testimony of the distant past and show the sculptor's first attempts to depict the human likeness in carved stone. These colossal works were supposed to represent King Djoser as Osiris. The mummiform figure holding a scepter is swathed in a tight-fitting cloak and wears the ceremonial beard.

Historians disagree on the exact location of this land of spices; some claim that it was situated in Abyssinia near the Horn of Africa, others place it across the Red Sea in the southwestern region of the Arabian peninsula.

## Social discipline

During the Archaic Period, people fled the Sahara region that was progressively drying out and turning into a desert. They found refuge in the Nile Valley along the banks of the river and in the Delta. This growing population provided the millions of laborers needed to control the challenging physical environment of the annual flood. Indeed, the erratic and unpredictable inundation must have been an awesome threat for primitive settlers. Artificial hills were built to keep the villages above water level; dikes were raised to control flooding and to allow the population to move from one place to another; canals were dug to drain the marshes and irrigate the desert fringes. The early inhabitants of the Nile Valley had to undertake what would now be called a massive regional development program.

Such tasks required a high degree of coordination and called for a strong centralized government, as well as hard-line collective discipline. Villagers had to be fully aware of their involvement in a larger community. Local chieftains acquired the ability to carry out ambitious projects planned by higher authorities and conducted large teams of laborers with utmost efficiency. The fulfillment of these conditions explains the emergence of architectural achievements such as the impressive Predynastic buildings and funerary monuments.

## From silt to carved rock

Instinctively, the first builders made use of the silt from the Nile. The peasants *(fellahs)* made the walls of their dwellings out of bundles of reeds coated with a mixture of chopped straw and argillaceous mud often extracted from a near-by irrigation ditch. They covered their dwellings with roofs of palm fronds which provided protection from the fiery sun and from extremes of temperature. This wattle-and-daub construction was well-suited to a rainless climate, and silt–the basic construction material–was generously supplied by the annual floods.

When the ancient Egyptians felt the urgent need to protect their dead from decay, simple graves were no longer adequate. What they required were large enough burial places to hold a body preserved by rudimentary mummification methods as well as a few offerings meant to pay for the journey to the Great Beyond. The tombs now consisted of an underground funeral chamber for the deceased and storage rooms covered by a simple mound which served to mark the burial site. This increasingly colossal bench-like superstructure, called a mastaba, had to be strong enough to resist the pressure of an enormous mass of sand blown by desert storms. At first, a sundried mudbrick construction was sufficient; later on hardier materials were used and new techniques devised.

Building with bricks of the same length, width and breadth soon replaced the banking up of shapeless mud; a kind of standardization resulted followed by a process of prefabrication. Furthermore, mudbrick structures needed systematic planning, for the design of a wall depended on how the courses were laid one on top of the other, on how headers and stretchers alternated, and on how the joints were made. Such practices brought Egyptian architects to devise a modular system of construction based on proportions which were derived from foot and cubit measurements.

Nilotic builders learned many design principles from the elemental mudbrick technique, such as geometrical regularity based on the repetition of right angles. From the Fourth Millennium BC on, an orthogonal feeling for space played a fundamental role in Egyptian architecture, as it also did in Sumerian and Elamite civilizations. In Egypt, early mortuary monuments were based on rectangularity; recesses and salient angles gave a rhythm to walls and were suggestive of a fortress-like prototype, for example the girdle walls surrounding the first royal city–the famous White Walls of Memphis. The so-called "palace façade" design with a series of false doors flanked by towers and bastions, derived from the mudbrick exterior of early buildings.

Before the start of the Third Millennium BC, during the Thinite Period, mortuary monuments reached considerable dimensions with lengths of 150 to 180ft (50 to 60m) and widths of 75 to 90ft (25 to 30m). In order to assert their control over the Two Lands, the early kings had funerary monuments built in both Lower and Upper Egypt, for example the cenotaphs at Abydos (memorials commemorating the ancestors of the early pharaohs) and tombs at Saqqara (the burial grounds of the city of Memphis) with their elaborate decor and rich furnishings.

**Prehistoric stone vessel.**

About 40,000 stone vessels were concealed in subterranean chambers under King Djoser's Step Pyramid. These beautiful objects came down from the king's ancestors. Carved out of very hard stone such as diorite or granite, they bear witness to the mastery achieved by craftsmen as early as the Archaic Period. (Musée du Louvre, Paris)

**The Bull Palette.**

This slate palette dating from between 3500 and 3100 BC is an accomplished work symbolizing power. It shows a mighty bull goring an Asian enemy. The emblems of five of the provinces (*nomes*) are depicted by hands hauling on a rope and probably represent a pact signed between allies. (Musée du Louvre, Paris)

**The hauling of an Egyptian colossus.**

This bas-relief from a Middle Kingdom tomb at Beni Hasan was drawn by von Minutoli, a German traveler, and published in 1823. A careful analysis of the scene shows how the monolithic statue of a seated pharaoh, about 26ft high (8m), was securely tied with ropes to a wooden sledge. Four teams, each of about twenty-four laborers, haul ropes to move the huge load. A foreman stands on the colossus, synchronizing the action by rhythmically clapping his hands. An assistant pours water to wet the argillaceous silt so that the runners can slide more easily. Below, three men carry water in goatskins balanced on poles, and three others transport a wooden stepladder. Fifteen team leaders wait behind the statue, while six dozen wardens, holding rods and maces, stand ready to coax a maximum effort out of the work force. Thus, 172 people were needed to skillfully move a statue measuring some 2650 cubic feet (75 cubic meters) and weighing approximately 220 tons (200 metric tons).

In some cases, the ceilings, floors and walls of the tombs were dressed with wooden paneling; but, as the durability of wood was questioned, the builders turned to fine limestone to face the coarser materials. Granite was used for doorframes and, as early as the Second Dynasty (c. 3000 BC), the huge plugs *(portculles)* that barred access to the subterranean chambers were made out of the same hard stone.

Thousands of beautiful stone vessels have been discovered in storage rooms excavated under mastabas. Carved with utmost precision, these vessels in alabaster or limestone as well as in hard stones such as diorite, granite and schist attest to the exceptional mastery of Egyptian craftsmen. These ancestral techniques can be traced back to the prehistoric stone carving of flintstone artifacts and were perfected over the centuries as demonstrated by the extremely crisp cutting of reliefs on archaic slate palettes that already show most of the fundamental characteristics of pharaonic art.

After a long period of experimentation that lasted until the beginning of the Third Dynasty (c. 2800 BC), the art and architecture of Ancient Egypt were ready to come into their own. Techniques and artistic schemes had been thoroughly tested and now after centuries of effort the time was ripe for more daring creations.

### The "divine" Imhotep invents stone architecture

The talented Imhotep conceived a vast complex for King Djoser at Saqqara on the west bank of the Nile near Memphis, at the edge of the desert plateau in Lower Egypt. This necropolis served as a substitute city for the dead and had a magical purpose. Here, the deceased king could enjoy an infinitely more beautiful, and more unalterable environment in which to rest for eternity than that of the palace at Memphis, where he had lived as a mortal.

Prehistoric Egypt went through a cultural evolution that stretched over many millennia, from the early Neolithic Age to the time of King Djoser, the first great ruler of the Third Dynasty. During this long period before the invention of writing, the ancient Egyptian master-builders seemed to have gone through a phase of apprenticeship. They progressively acquired the maturity needed to produce masterpieces. Although the process appears to have taken place suddenly, this impression is due to an erroneous perception of time.

Opposite, top:

**Sculptors at work, copied from a wall-painting of the New Kingdom Period.**

This scene shows sculptors carving, polishing, and adding a finishing touch to two granite colossi, one seated, and one standing, and to a limestone sphinx. This drawing is a copy of a wall-painting in the tomb of Rekhmire at Sheikh abd el-Qurna (Western Thebes) dating from the Eighteenth Dynasty (c. 1500-1300 BC) made by the Egyptologist Richard Lepsius. The ancient Egyptians showed great concern for the skills and techniques demonstrated by their craftsmen.

Opposite, lower left:

**Two sculptors carving wooden Djed-Pillars.**

Seated on stools, the craftsmen use adzes to roughhew their work placed on wooden blocks. This scene from a Theban tomb was copied by Rosellini and published in 1832.

Opposite, lower right:

**A cabinetmaker leveling a plank.**

A craftsman surrounded by a handsome cambered-top chest and the various tools of his trade: an adze planted in a wood block and various instruments for squaring and trying angles. This scene was also reproduced by Rosellini.

The evolution of construction techniques from prehistoric shelters established along the annually flooded Nile Valley and the huts of later dwellings made of reeds and palm ferns coated with mud demonstrate the Egyptians' concern with eternity and their continual search for more permanent types of building. The mudbrick bastioned walls, characteristic of Predynastic-Age mastabas, announced more permanent all-stone structures; in fact, the first stone constructions were made of small blocks resembling bricks.

In accordance with the Egyptian religious precepts, the deified architect strove to preserve King Djoser's necropolis from decay by using stone as his medium. He designed a girdle wall with a majestic entrance enclosing a step pyramid surrounded by shrines. The whole complex was built out of quarried stones over a maze of subterranean chambers. But most of the above-ground constructions were mere solid dummies without inner rooms, displaying stone imitations of wooden doors, false stake fences, and engaged columns having no structural function. All these artifices were intended to serve merely as a decor.

At Saqqara, craftsmen elaborated sophisticated settings, mastered stone construction with carefully squared blocks, and discovered the art of volumetric carving of statues (*stereotomy*) at one go (*c.* 2800 BC). The basic principles of pharaonic art were thus set and underwent only minor stylistic variations during rest of the life-span of Egyptian civilization. Egyptian architecture appeared to emerge complete with all its stylistic features such as stem-like lotus columns, papyrus capitals, elements based on plant forms, slab abaci, fluted shafts, bastioned walls, cambered roofs, fan-shaped cavetto cornices, stone imitations of wooden ceilings, friezes with the cobra motif *(uraeus)*, reliefs displaying ritual scenes and funerary statues portraying the deceased.

This formal repertory continued to inspire Egyptian master-builders and invigorate the art of building for thousands of years to come heralding the Doric column, the porticos of Greek temples, and Hellenic military architecture of some twenty-two centuries later.

## Petrified architecture

The stone buildings at Saqqara were equivalent to the mudbrick structures of older times and derived directly from the brickwork of the Thinite mastabas. The walls consisted of a rubble core faced with carefully cut limestone blocks, a method recalling the older technique

34

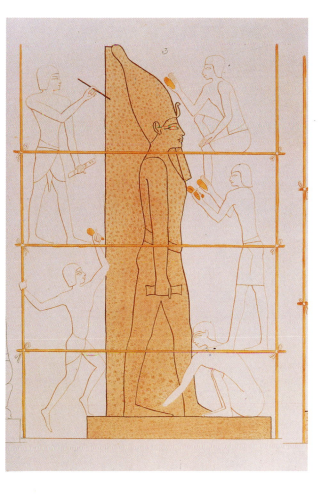

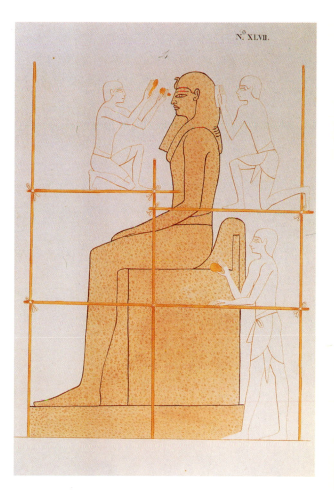

**Giving the finishing touches to granite colossi.**

Rosellini copied these two scenes from the same tomb subsequently studied by Richard Lepsius. They depict sculptors perched on light scaffolding polishing statues.

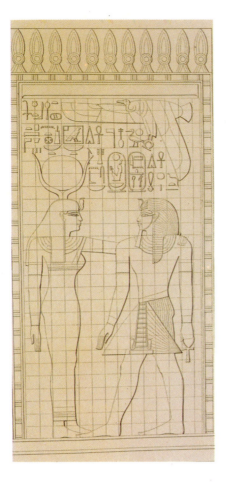

**A sketch drawn for Amenophis III's tomb.**

This scene of the king led by the beautiful goddess Hathor was simply sketched out, first in red chalk and then with pen and ink. The drawing is overlaid with a square grid for transfer to a larger scale.


Opposite:

**The square grid, an accurate method of reproduction.**

Different wall-paintings found in unfinished tombs describe methods used by Egyptians to obtain a larger version of a composition. This elegant silhouette and the one above belong to a New Kingdom tomb at El Kab–formerly called Nekhen–where the vulture goddess Nekhbet was worshipped. This drawing, reproduced by Richard Lepsius, displays the outstanding skill of Egyptian artists and shows how they followed strict stylistic conventions.

of building walls with fine baked bricks set around a core of coarser sun-dried bricks. This process can be described as the petrifaction of a system of construction that already belonged to the past.

The stonework used at Saqqara derived from the brickwork of the Thinite mastabas and consisted of dressed blocks smoothly finished and carefully squared, laid in regular horizontal courses. The size of the stone blocks was very similar to that of the mudbricks and limited the height of the walls. It took a certain amount of time for Egyptian master-builders to realize that increasing the volume of the blocks brought more stability and allowed them to build taller structures. Furthermore, raising monuments in this way was faster, since less time was spent dressing, carving and squaring the stones. The discovery of this basic principle led to ever more ambitious creations, such as King Khephren's Lower Temple near Giza (Old Kingdom) with its colossal monolithic pillars.

In order to achieve an architecture as revolutionary as the one he had created for King Djoser, Imhotep had to solve many technical problems. Excavations and reconstruction carefully conducted by archeologist Jean-Philippe Lauer of the Institut Français d'Archéologie Orientale of Cairo has revealed how the extraordinary master-builder experimented through a process of trial and error.

Petrifaction was a turning-point in the history of architecture; apparently, the girdle wall at Saqqara renewed with the familiar palace-façade pattern of an earlier period (First Dynasty), but transposed the formula onto a much grander scale. The enclosure, built on a rectangular ground plan and accurately oriented toward the cardinal points, measures 1768ft (544m) from north to south and 900ft (277m) from east to west; the wall is 20 cubits (34ft/10.5m) high; the perimeter–more than a mile long–encloses an area of 37 acres (15 hectares). Within this vast *temenos* rose the famous step tomb, the first Egyptian pyramid.

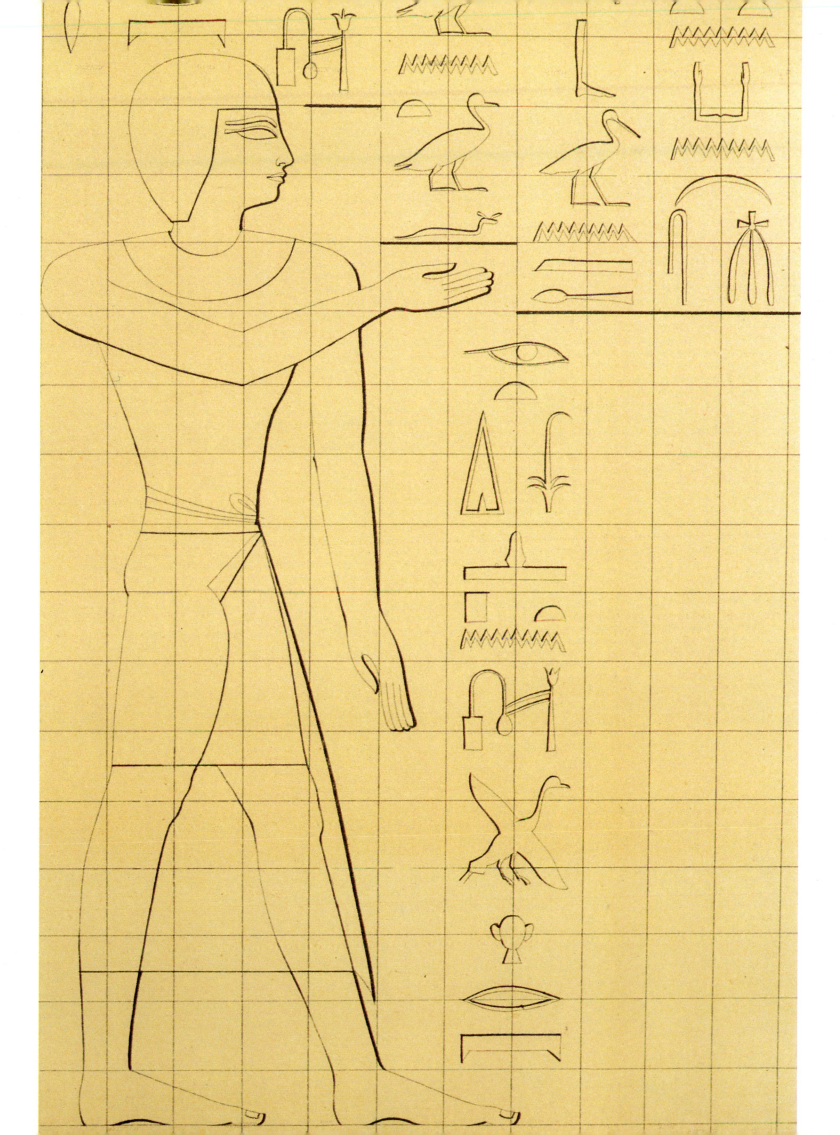

# THE AGE
# OF THE GREAT PYRAMIDS

*The gigantic structures built at Giza–the great Pyramids
of Kings Khephren and Mykerinus–attest
to the formidable energy expended by the Egyptians
to express their belief in an afterlife.*

The first Egyptian pyramid worthy of the name though still imperfect was erected during the Third Dynasty under King Djoser. This type of structure was intended to house and protect the dead body of the deified pharaoh and fulfilled a very important role in the funerary art of the Old Kingdom. Although pyramids indeed continued to flourish during the Fourth Dynasty, the pyramidal structure–symbol of pharaonic art in all its massiveness and geometrical perfection–can best be understood through a careful study of Imhotep's previous creation at Saqqara.

It is interesting to speculate on what really took place during the construction of the Step Pyramid which proudly rises above the desert sands. It would seem that Imhotep's original objective was merely to build a huge mastaba inside

Opposite:

**The great Pyramid of Khephren at the edge of the desert, seen from the top of the Pyramid of Kheops.**

Built around 2650 BC by Khephren, the second of Giza's pyramids culminates at 471ft (143.5m); the sides of the square base are 706ft (215.2m) long. On the tip of the pyramid some of the limestone casing that once clad the whole structure can still be seen. Kheops reaches the height of 481ft (146.6m), on a base of 756ft (230.3m) or 100 cubits. The volume of this great pyramid is about 92 million cubic feet (2.6 million cubic meters) representing more than 7 million tons of stone entirely transported without benefit of machinery.

**The base of the Pyramid
of King Mykerinus, the third
of Giza's pyramids.**

The smaller proportions of the
Pyramid of King
Mykerinus–less than 203ft
(62m) high and 354ft (108m)
wide–announced the decrease
in the size of monuments
toward the end of the Old
Kingdom. On the east side,
some of the granite ashlars
from Aswan that once clad the
whole structure can be seen
laid in perfectly horizontal
courses. This pyramid was
built with an angle of 52°,
while the angle for Kheops
angle is 51°52', and for the
steeper Khephren's, 52°20'.

the stone walls of a rectangular precinct. The bench-like
superstructure forming the nucleus of the Step Pyramid,
with its battered sides and cambered top, was erected over a
complex of burial chambers and storage rooms hewn out of
the rock, some of them at a depth of 92ft (28m) below
ground.

The initial mastaba was built of stone on a square ground
plan, each side measuring about 205ft (62.5m), and rose to a
height of 26ft (7.9m). The monument then underwent many
plan modifications and eventually became a structure with
four levels reaching a height of about 140ft (42m) above the
ground. Ultimately, the whole base of the structure was
extended north and west to form a quadrangular base (397 x
358ft; 121 x 109m) for a white stone pyramid with six
unequal steps culminating at approximately 200ft (60m),
totaling some 9 millions cubic feet (260,000 cubic meters) of
stonework. It resembled a giant staircase climbing skyward.

## Toward perfect form

This preliminary exploit, followed by several unfinished
attempts, announced the advent of the Age of the Great
Pyramids, between 2700 and 2600 BC and the accomplishments of the great master-builders: Kings Snoferu, Kheops,
and Khephren. The first true pyramid set on a square base,
with four equal triangular faces converging to a single point
at apex, was built by King Snoferu, when the pharaoh was
established at Meydum. Although it fell into a state of ruin, it
was a major achievement in its day. It appears that this
structure did not grow out of a mastaba like the Step
Pyramid but was conceived from the start as a mathematic-
ally perfect three-dimensional pyramid-shaped figure. A
mantle of granite ashlars clad the step-structured core, giving
the monument a smooth appearance. Although in a state of
ruin today, it was a fundamental achievement. Its origins are
disputed; although it is generally attributed to King Snoferu,
the father of King Kheops, the Egyptologist Jean-Paul Lauer
believes that its construction began under Snoferu's father,
King Huni, and that Snoferu only added the granite casing.

King Snoferu also had two other colossal pyramids built
in South and North Dahshur. These royal undertakings
marked the apogee of the classic pyramid and set new
standards in the conduction of gigantic building and
engineering projects.

The first of these pyramids, the Bent Pyramid at South
Dahshur–sometimes incorrectly called the Rhomboidal
Pyramid–represents an intermediate form. Halfway up, at

about 164ft (50m), the slope of the sides was made less steep; the angle of incline was changed from 54°27' to 43°22'. The junction of the two differently inclined surfaces of stonework formed a sharp ridge in the casing. Some experts think that the builders of the Bent Pyramid were forced to limit the height of the structure when several cracks began to appear during the construction. Had this pyramid been finished according to the slope originally planned, it would have reached a height of 420ft (128m). This change of inclination restricted the final height to a more modest 328ft (100m). Another explanation is based on the double nature of the Bent Pyramid, for it was built over two independent burial chambers. One was reached from the north and was carved out of the rock to a depth of 82ft (25m). The other, accessed from the west, lay even deeper below the base of the pyramid 98ft (30m). The two pyramids, each corresponding to a tomb, were fused together into a single structure. Had the lower pyramid's edges had been extended direct to an apex, it would have been extremely high. On the other hand, if the edges of the higher pyramid had been extended downwards it would have generated a flatter pyramid on a square base with a side of 690ft (210m). Curiously enough, the two structures would have had about the same volume-53 million cubic feet (1.5 million cubic meters).

The pyramid at North Dahshur is supposed to have been the last one built by King Snoferu. Its triangular faces rise on a square base of 722ft (220m) to the side. The apex is only 328ft (100m) above ground. This pyramid was built with a relatively low angle of inclination of 43°40', while the Kheops Pyramid had a slope with an angle of 51°52' and rose to 481ft (146.6m) on a square base 756ft (230.3m) to the side. Its volume amounted to some 88 millions cubic feet (2.5 million cubic meters).

At Giza, the precision—greater than 10 minutes of angle (one sixth of a degree)—with which the pyramids were oriented to the cardinal points is prodigious. The sides of these geometrical three-dimensional figures are perfectly plane isosceles triangles.

All these measurements give us an idea of the extraordinary achievements of the Fourth Dynasty. It is as if the art of colossal building had been mastered in one fell swoop, producing grandiose and everlasting monuments that have had no equivalent anywhere else in the world. By that time, Egyptian building techniques had reached their highest level of perfection and the construction of giant pyramids—accomplished through the efforts an

**The Valley Temple of King Khephren.**

The lower part of the causeway linking the valley temple to the Pyramid of King Khephren at Giza, with its red granite blocks from Aswan, marks the apogee of Cyclopean masonry.

Opposite. One of the three naves of the Valley Temple. Each row is composed of five monolithic square piers, built according to the very ancient post-and-lintel system of construction (*trilithon*), with two piers supporting massive monolithic architraves. The stone slabs of the ceiling have disappeared. The severe forms tempered by the elegant proportions impart an austere classicism to the building.

**The Great Sphinx at Giza. King Khephren represented by a giant reclining lion with a human head.**

Sculpted from an outcrop of limestone on the plateau north of the Valley Temple of Khephren below the pyramid; this colossal head of the King wearing the striped headcloth (*nemes*) was found buried in the sand up to the neck (photograph taken in 1864).

Opposite. The excavated Sphinx, a representation of Re-Horakhte (Horus, the sun as it stands above the Horizon) awaits restoration. Between its two huge paws (already restored) stands an altar and a stela on which an inscription relates a dream that King Tuthmosis IV had a thousand years after the Sphinx's completion: he heard the voice of Harmachis beseeching him to extricate the monument, a task that he scrupulously performed.

**The King Mykerinus triad, example of hieratic statuary from the Old Kingdom.**

This flawless work of schist, measuring about three feet high and dating from 2600 BC, shows the deified king flanked on the left by the goddess Hathor, Mother of the Heavens, bearing the sun-disk between cows horns on her head. On the right, the Land of the Nile is personified by a goddess who symbolizes the Seventeenth Nome of Upper Egypt. The bodies of the women tightly clad in clinging drapery hides nothing of their beauty. The King is wearing the White Crown and a pleated loincloth. (Egyptian Museum, Cairo)

entire nation–had attained their zenith. Khephren and Mykerinus persevered in this endeavor, for the colossal proportions of pyramids only began to take on more modest proportions in the Fifth and Sixth Dynasties.

A great many questions arise concerning these marvelous works which confound the senses of all who approach them. What was the purpose of these buildings, their meaning? How were they conceived, planned, and built? How were the materials transported? Who composed the work force that labored on these construction sites four and a half millennia ago?

The pharaonic pyramids, for all their magnitude, represented merely the center of a vast complex. The mortal remains of the pharaoh, brought by boat, were received and prepared in a valley temple built along a canal connected to the river with landing docks and piers. This lower sanctuary was linked by a paved and covered inclined causeway measuring several hundred meters long to the foot of the pyramid. Here, an upper sanctuary served as an offering chamber for the cult of the dead king. The complex also included a warren of inner corridors, corbel-vaulted chambers, apartments, and storehouses. After all the mortuary rituals had been accomplished, the mummified body was sealed inside the pyramid which then became the eternal residence of the sovereign.

## The significance of the pyramid shape

The symbolic meaning of the pyramid's shape has always aroused a great deal of interest, and many different explanations have been advanced. Most likely its form evolved from a simple cone-shaped tumulus of sand accumulated on top of a tomb. At a certain point, the tumulus was given a square base and sharp edges and turned into a geometrical figure. Pyramids also performed the same function as the sacred *ben-ben* stone, a pyramidal or conical object probably of meteoric origin, which was revered in the city of Heliopolis. Pyramids and obelisks can be considered large-scale models of this sacred stone. Another possibility is that the triangular shape gave a somewhat apprehensible existence to the rays of the sun and resembled giant stairs leading to the heavens toward Re, the Sun-God. The Sun Temple of Niuserre at Heliopolis (Fifth Dynasty, *c.* 2500 BC), as well as the stone obelisks which were erected as early as the reign of Pepi I (Sixth Dynasty) are perfect examples of this type of symbolism.

These structures offered a place of exchange between

**The burial chamber in the Pyramid of King Unas; the walls are covered with the Pyramid Texts.**

The last king of the Fifth Dynasty (c. 2450 BC) introduced the practice of writing long hieroglyphic inscriptions on the walls of the burial chamber. This body of texts, spells, incantations, and sayings were designed to ensure the well-being of the king in his next life. The two sides of the saddleback roof are covered with stars. In the center, the sarcophagus where the king was put to rest.

**Wooden headrest from the Old Kingdom displaying the elegance of ordinary household objects.**

From a tomb discovered in 1911 by the Italian Egyptologist Schiaparelli at the Gebelein site in Upper Egypt, this piece of furniture dates from the Fifth Dynasty (c. 2450 BC). This type of object, also used in Black Africa, replaced cushions that were impractical in hot weather. Carved in precious wood, this one displays a particular grace.
The craftsman gave the most ordinary objects of everyday life a quality that demonstrates the aesthetic perfectionism of the population as a whole.
(Museo Egizio, Turin)

the earthbound world and the celestial universe with its immortal heavenly bodies into which the resuscitated pharaoh would be reborn to rise and sit on the right hand of his father, Re, as it is written in the *Pyramid Texts.* The triangular masses with their gilded peaks pointing toward the sky were a sort of Jacob's ladder providing a passage for messengers from the realm of the gods.

Toward the end of the Fifth Dynasty, the pyramids began to serve as receptacles for ancient magico-religious texts that covered the walls of the sepulchral chambers. These *Pyramid Texts* contain the oldest sacred traditions that have come down to us and stand as the first great creations of hieroglyphic writing. They are a compilation of spells, incantations, utterances, and sacred formulas designed to ensure the dead king's well-being in his next life and to reconcile him with the gods. These texts are all too often impossible to decipher because they underwent so many alterations due to their oral transmission over long periods of time. The pyramids of Unas, Teti, Pepi I and Merenre at Saqqara all preserve these great litanies that guaranteed a safe passage to the Great Beyond.

## Building methods

Following Imhotep's first ingenious attempts in stone construction, Egyptian architects mastered the handling of ever greater volumes and were able to progressively enlarge the size of the stone blocks thus raising increasingly gigantic structures. For example, the Kheops Pyramid is composed of 10 million blocks of fine-grained limestone from the quarries of Tura and Mokkatam (the site of present-day Cairo) representing a total volume of 90 million cubic feet (2.5 million cubic meters). The lower courses were made of stone blocks of about 50 cubic feet (1.5 cubic meters) each; the size of the blocks decreased to about 17 cubic feet (0.5 cubic meters) at the summit.

Exactly how the Egyptians quarried, cut, and transported such a volume of stone to the plateau of Giza still remains a mystery today. At the time of the Fourth Dynasty, the process was all the more difficult as they did not have wheels strong enough to bear heavy loads, nor domestic animals to pull them, nor any lifting devices such as cranes or hoists .

In the quarries, the workers would split off large pieces of limestone by inserting wedges of dry wood into small holes punched into the surface of the rock, to form a sort of dotted line; when wet the wedges would expand, breaking off large pieces of rock which were then cut into

**Wall-painting copied by Richard Lepsius in a tomb of the Fourth Dynasty at Giza.**

Many of the Memphite tombs excavated by the French Egyptologist Mariette and others before him were covered over again with sand for security. Here, the deceased was a priest, indicated by his panther-skin garment whose spots symbolized stars. This figure appears several times on the wall: seated in front of a table bearing offerings, above the false door and on both sides of this scene. The central figure carrying a mace and a long cane–insignia of his rank–is inspecting the goods being brought to him by servants and peasants.

**False door to Princess Uhemnofret's tomb at Giza, Fifth Dynasty.**

The drum between the jambs of the false door is part of the stereotypical decor. The name and titles of the deceased are carved on the lintel. On the panel (tympanum) above, the princess is shown seated at an offering table. Reliefs on each side depict offering-bearers. (Museo Egizio, Turin)

Opposite:

**The main offering-chamber in Mereruka's Mastaba at Saqqara.**

Dating from the reign of King Teti (c. 2450 BC) this vast funerary complex was built for a high-priest who had married a royal daughter and consisted of no less than 32 rooms. On the left, the statue of Mereruka, also known as Meri, occupies a niche in the wall. Pictures of the deceased wearing the panther skin, insignia of his priesthood, are carved on the pillars.

**Statue of Renofer, High Priest of Ptah.**

This (727/8in; 180cm ) painted limestone statue from the Fifth Dynasty (c. 2520 BC) was found in Renofer's mastaba at Saqqara. Representing the apogee of private statuary during the Old Kingdom, this idealized portrayal shows a strong, determined, and athletic man. (Egyptian Museum, Cairo)

smaller blocks of equal size. The craftsmen used a variety of different tools for cutting, such as hammers and instruments made of flint, hard stone, or copper. The finished blocks were transported to the site by boats and barges to the piers of the valley temples along the Nile.

Teams of laborers harnessed to sledges dragged the blocks over a layer of silt always kept moist so that the runners would slide. The blocks were pulled up a series of ramps toward the desert plateau in the same fashion. Little by little as the pyramid grew the blocks would have to be hauled up to a higher level. There are contradictory and complementary hypotheses to explain this operation. Lauer has suggested that a large ramp of dried brick was simultaneously constructed against one side of the pyramid. As the ramp had to rise in height too, it would have had to attain a width of a hundred meters and a length of 1300 to 1650ft (400 to 500m) which represented a third of the volume of the pyramid itself, and it would have been very costly both in material and energy. In the end, the ramp would have to be taken down. No trace of this method of construction have never been found, even on the unfinished pyramids.

Other Egyptologists have supposed that a helical brick ramp gradually enveloping the pyramid. With this method however, the ancient engineers would have faced a major difficulty: how to slide the blocks over the sharp angles of the pyramid. This problem could have been solved by constructing large platforms at all four corners of the edifice, thus enabling the crews to maneuver the blocks. This would also have permitted the installation of the granite ashlars that clad the entire façade; the workmen could have gradually dressed and polished the casing, starting at the summit and working toward the base, taking down the brick ramp along the way. This latter technique seems the more plausible, for it corresponds to documented accounts of the construction of the pylon gateway of the temples of the New Kingdom.

It should be noted also that the inner chambers of the great pyramids were covered with immense ashlars of Aswan granite weighing tens of tons. Buried deep within the pyramid directly above the burial chamber, a high chamber ensuring the even distribution of pressure required stone lintels whose enormous span must have presented great problems to architects operating without benefit of lifting devices.

If the work had used slave labor, as was claimed in some late texts, this would have affected the quality of the construction. Such perfection must have required an unshakable determination and patient team work, as well

Previous page:

**Standing at the feet of her master, Mereruka accompanies the deceased in his tomb.**

This elegant feminine silhouette holding a lotus flower is clad in a close-fitting linen dress with straps and is represented in a smaller scale indicating lower rank.

Below:

**Funerary Barque of King Kheops, vestige of the remarkable Egyptian boat-building techniques at the time of the Old Kingdom.**

This 143ft (43.6m) vessel was discovered in a dismantled state at the foot of the Great Pyramid in 1954; it was entirely rebuilt from the wooden elements that had been found deposited in a large trench dug out of the rock. The cedar strakes were attached with knotted cords, as the use of ribs was unknown. Neither nails nor rivets were used in the construction.

as absolute faith in the redeeming role of the pharaoh-god. For this reason, it may be presumed that the sovereign availed himself of his peasant work force, that was left inactive during the dry season. Construction therefore took place during the months that followed the harvest and before the onslaught of the much-awaited flood. Then teams of laborers worked in exchange for food that was stocked in the King's granaries. This system functioned like a kind of insurance scheme to prevent grain speculation during the years of famine and want.

### Art and the funerary complex

The Egyptian master-builders were not just engaged in building pyramids and we have already seen examples of valley and upper temples joined to the pyramids by covered causeways. The lower sanctuary near the Sphinx in the Khephren complex was almost entirely preserved over the centuries beneath the sand, such that today we can see the great hall of the temple with its rows of monolithic piers of red granite supporting massive architraves, a perfect example of the post and lintel technique *(trilithon)*. The edifice was obliquely lit from above thanks to a series of louvers along the line of the ceiling revealing diorite, granite, alabaster, schist and limestone statues of the pharaoh, standing or seated on a throne and often combined with groups of triple deities *(triads)*.

Reliefs and texts from the great period of pharaonic architecture also attest to a coherent "Egyptian style" with all its characteristic features: a combination of geometry, symmetry, and clever observation of nature that was found in all Egyptian art. The reliefs displayed voluntary distortions so that figures appeared complete in their most typical aspect; for example, the head was most easily recognizable in profile, the torso from the front, but arms and feet in motion were more efficiently represented sideways. The Nilotic artist strove to depict the attributes which he knew belonged to a person or a scene. Examples of the rules and conventions governing Egyptian stereotypical representation first appeared on Predynastic slate palettes used for grinding cosmetics and then, on King Djoser's stelae during the Fourth and Fifth Dynasties (between 2700 and 2400 BC). None of these works however was intended to be enjoyed as an art object but aspired to represent an eternal truth.

On occasion, large barques—either whole or in pieces—were set at the foot of the royal sarcophagi. Two boats built for King Kheops were discovered in 1954, one of which was

**Shipbuilding required cedarwood from Lebanon.**

The elegant curved stern and the beautiful stempost of this barque demonstrate the skill of early Egyptian shipwrights. The cabin could house passengers or precious freight during trips on the Nile. For navigation on the open sea, larger barges with higher broadsides must have been built. Below. Before reassembling the barque, a model was made at a scale of 1:10, complete with the hull, the ten rowing oars, the two steering oars, and the canopy to protect the crew, oarsmen, and passengers from the scorching sun. It was easier for the archeologists to manipulate the parts of a maquette—each one a perfect replica of the original element—than the forty-seven-century-old strakes weighing two or three tons apiece.

**The deceased welcoming offerings at the entrance of a tomb.**

The owner of the tomb, sculpted on one of the jambs of the false door leading to the funerary chapel, wears a broad necklace, and holds a long cane and a mace. Part of the mace is hidden behind the figure, confusing with the position of the arm.

later re-assembled in a museum. Sometimes described as a "solar barque," this river vessel was actually used in funeral ceremonies to transport the deceased and all his lavish belongings from the east to the west bank of the Nile where he would be lain to rest for eternity in the House of the Dead. The wooden boat, approximately 143ft (43m) long, was made out of superb Lebanon cedar and demonstrates the skill of Egyptian naval architects at the time. The trees needed for boat building did not grow in Egypt, and we know that as early as King Snoferu, expeditions of dozens of vessels brought back wood from Phoenicia.

## The necropoles of the nobles

Saqqara and Giza were true Cities of the Dead. Mortuary shrines devoted to the nobles of the royal household lined the streets of the necropolis in the vicinity of the pyramids under the protection of the pharaoh-god. The inner walls of these mastabas were adorned with animated reliefs and paintings subtly narrating the circumstances in which the tomb owner desired to be remembered. The figurative repertory evoked the daily chores of craftsmen and peasants, hunting expeditions in the bulrushes, or religious offerings and sacrifices that evoked the noble's everyday activities and which he hoped to continue forever in the Afterlife.

The scenes described by the hieroglyphic texts carved on the walls of the tombs mentioned the deeds of the nobles for whom these eternal edifices were constructed, commemorated certain biographical events, enumerated gifts and offerings, and prescribed ritual gestures. They spread across the chambers like an immense papyrus scroll mingling scripture and illustration. Laborers, plowmen, reapers, grape pickers, carpenters and boat-builders performed their tasks; sculptors and goldsmiths plied their trade, while processions of servants bore gifts. On one wall were shown animals raised for butchering, and on another the wild animals that were hunted in the desert. Elsewhere, dozens of workmen were shown dragging a colossus, others making furniture and precious boxes. Although intended for the dead, the decoration of these tombs was actually a great hymn to life.

It was imperative that the deceased have all his needs met, whether a guardian, a servant, or a mistress. From the Middle Kingdom on, small statuettes *(ushabtis)*, each marked with a name and a profession, were placed near the mummy in symbolic readiness to carry out the tasks which the deceased might require of them. These figures and

models provided him with helpmates that would be resurrected with him and allow him to make his appearance in the other world with a suitable retinue. This population of servants subject to the will of their all-powerful master, could be counted in the hundreds in some of the tombs, indicating by their number the rank of the occupant.

Here we are faced with a paradox; from ancient Egyptian civilization, only the houses of the dead have survived and yet these funerary monuments testify to a joy of life which stands in complete contrast to their actual contents: coffins and mummies.

**Rural scene from an Old Kingdom tomb at Saqqara.**

A herd of oxen with lyre-shaped horns ford a river in which a hippopotamus and various species of fish swim. This panel from the mastaba of the vizier Kagemni, with its sharp rendition of animal life and vigorously designed hieroglyphs, is a good example of Fifth Dynasty art.

**A beautiful wall-painting copied in 1842 by Richard Lepsius from an tomb Old Kingdom at Giza.**

This Fifth Dynasty panel represents the deceased clad in the cat-skin worn by priests, seated on a stool with animal-shaped legs in front of a table laden with loaves of bread. Various foodstuffs abound in dishes and platters along with drinking vessels and haunches of venison brought by servants comprise the viaticum for the deceased's journey to the Beyond.

**Limestone relief from the Mastaba of King Huti (Fifth Dynasty) in Saqqara.**

This sculpted panel. contemporary with the preceding , illustrates the deceased in a seated position counting the offerings that he is providing for his wife Ketisen (not shown in this detail). She is seated facing him in front of a table laden with bread. Huti wears a complicated wig and a long robe attached at the left shoulder by a large bow. Each ligature of the animal-leg stool is rendered in perfect detail. (Egyptian Museum, Cairo)

# COLLAPSE,
# REVOLUTION AND RENAISSANCE
# DURING THE MIDDLE KINGDOM

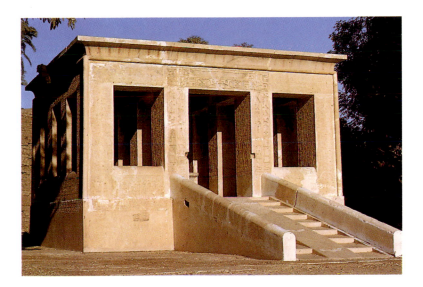

*This austere repository of the Sacred Barque is*
*a paragon of Middle Kingdom architecture.*

The Old Kingdom covered a time span of about 500 years (from 2700 to 2200 BC) ending in upheaval and revolt. At the end of the Sixth Dynasty a slow deterioration came about in the wake of the ineffectual reign of King Pepi II, who lived for more than a hundred years and occupied the throne for ninety-six of them. Insurrections raged unopposed leading to a progressive decline in authority and favoring the rise of a feudal state with local princes claiming independence for their provinces, or *nomes.* This caused the entire socio-political system to fall apart. The ingenious farming methods devised through generations of teamwork were abandoned, the canals were no longer kept up, and grain was no longer stored. Agricultural production decreased to such an extent that famine ensued.

Opposite:

**A classical masterpiece of Twelfth Dynasty architecture, recently rebuilt.**

Two shallow ramps give access to the small peripheral temple built in white limestone on a square ground plan, with angles bordered by torus moldings and sixteen pillars supporting a flat roof surmounted by a cavetto cornice. The small kiosk, known as the White Chapel, was constructed for the jubilee of King Sesostris I (c. 1940 BC). Later, under King Amenophis III, it was dismantled and the blocks were used as rubble to fill the core of the third pylon of the Temple of Amun. The Egyptologist Henri Chevrier was able to put together the pieces of this oversized puzzle when he rebuilt the kiosk in 1940.

Opposite:

**The raised reliefs inside the four-thousand-year-old kiosk of King Sesostris I.**

Carved on the pillars of the kiosk, ithyphallic representations of the god Min wearing a skullcap with two lofty plumes, raising his right arm, while holding the royal flail above his head with his hidden left arm. In the foreground, the granite plinth on which the priests laid the Sacred Barque on the day of the jubilee.

In just a few troubled decades, the central authority became too weak to quell the rising tide of anarchy, and Egypt split into a number of rival principalities. Now that the system rested on only a semblance of power and prosperity, widespread discontentment spread across the entire realm which was already in the throes of a bloody revolution.

Middle Kingdom texts narrate the horror of this tormented period when hordes of indigents attacked rich landowners, burned palaces, violated cenotaphs, plundered tombs of nobles, vandalized temples, pillaged pyramids, and made off with treasures, furniture, and jewelry. The insurgents even robbed the tombs containing their sovereigns' mummies which had been previously venerated as gods. Nothing resisted the fury of the angry crowds. The clever systems of protection were broken through; the many artifices such as false entrances, galleries with dead ends, and sliding portculles blocking the tomb shafts after burial were of no avail. All these stratagems did not discourage the robbers' avidity for the treasures stored in the royal tombs and mastabas. These hordes of desert nomads destroyed the Egyptians' sense of uniqueness and superiority and jeopardized the religious foundations of the Two Lands. The later texts relate these events in the form of prophesies—a literary convention subsequently in use up to the time of Isaiah and Jeremiah—and attest to the abominable tumult and violence into which Egypt was plunged.

This apocalyptic age and the tragic aftermath which ensued for almost two centuries form what historians call the First Intermediate Period, during which sovereigns overthrew each other in rapid succession through a series of indeterminate dynasties. From the Seventh to the Tenth Dynasty (c. 2250-2050 BC), the kings reigned only in name, and Lower, Middle, and Upper Egypt experienced a sort of feudalism at the hands of overlords.

### The restoration under King Mentuhotep

During the reign of Mentuhotep II-Nebhepetre a true renaissance flourished, bringing about the re-unification of the entire land, restoring peace and prosperity, encouraging artistic activity, and inciting the population to entrust their souls to the gods and their priests. The innovative sovereign resided in Thebes, the new capital of unified Egypt from the Eleventh to the Twelfth Dynasty. He had his own funerary temple erected in a dramatic

**This relief on the kiosk of King Sesostris I at Karnak shows a god leading the king into the temple and presenting the Sign of Life (*Ankh*) to his nostrils.**

The mastery displayed by this Middle Kingdom sculpture is so exceptional that we can only deplore the disappearance of most of the works from this period, a result of the destruction of the major temples.

Opposite:

**On another pillar of the kiosk, King Sesostris I holding libation vessels.**

The king, wearing the White Crown (*hedjet*) of Upper Egypt, offers fragrant ointments contained in libation vessels to Min, who was transformed from the god of animal fertility to the god of vegetation.

**Relief representing Achaït, the royal concubine of King Mentuhotep II.**

The concubine is wearing a wig, a close-fitting dress with narrow straps, a broad necklace with many strands, and bracelets at her wrist and ankles. She holds a lotus flower and an *ankh*. (Egyptian Museum, Cairo)

Opposite:

**A revolutionary achievement: the funerary Temple of King Mentuhotep II.**

The layout of the ruined Temple of King Mentuhotep II at Deir el-Bahri on the west bank of the Nile is still recognizable. A ramp led up to colonnades surrounding a three-level stepped mastaba. The hypostyle hall preceded a sanctuary hewn deeply in the mountainside (*hypogeum*). On the large forecourt the holes in which incense trees were planted are still visible.

setting formed by the Deir el-Bahri Hills in Western Thebes. The pyramid shape of the cliffs doubtless inspired the master-builder to develop a remarkably new concept in architecture. He constructed the extraordinary monument along an axis perpendicular to the hills, spreading the complex out on the plain before tunneling behind into the rock. The temple is in a state of ruin due to rock fall and because the stones were re-employed for other constructions over the centuries.

An imposing prospect, some 330ft (100m) in length, unfolded along gardens bordered with sacred trees. In the center a sloping ramp rose to a platform supporting a double row of 10 square pillars on each side, before continuing to a terrace bearing a second series of pillars. These were set in a U-shape around the third level. This girdle of 112 pillars—supplemented by 40 more along the lower façade for a total of 152—must have marked out the sides of a square that supported a central structure built in solid masonry. Archeologists have not been able to determine whether the structure was a pyramid or a flat-roofed mastaba.

Behind this vast terraced construction of nearly 750 square feet (70 square meters) lay a peristyle court surrounded by a roofed colonnade that led to the sacred hall—the inner sanctum—and was flanked by 88 proto-Doric octagonal columns. The protecting walls of this area of the temple were cut directly into the limestone cliff. From here, a 500-feet-long (150m) gallery led down to a chamber reserved for the royal sarcophagus.

This type of complex was reproduced throughout the New Kingdom; the funerary temples of Queen Hatshepsut and her successor Tuthmosis III, were erected on the same principle, with ramps, terraces, pillars and proto-Doric columns, as well as chambers dug into the hills.

### The return of the kings to Lower Egypt

For the Egyptians, however, restoration was not complete until their sovereigns returned to the city of Memphis, which occurred around 1990 BC during the Twelfth Dynasty. The Kings of the Middle Kingdom reinstated the great traditions of the Old Kingdom and once again began to erect pyramids for their burial grounds at Lisht in the Faiyum region and at Saqqara. Architectural techniques had certainly evolved but not always for the better. The pyramids, formed by diagonal walls with ramified series confusing chambers and

corridors, were built cheaply and hurriedly on poorly-consolidated foundations. To strengthen the interior, solid materials were compounded and then covered with a magnificent polished surface. The original stepped faces were too smooth to bind with the rubble mudbrick core, and not surprisingly, the Pyramid of Amenemhet collapsed during antiquity.

## The White Chapel

Unfortunately, only a few vestiges of the architecture from the Middle-Kingdom period remain. One edifice of exceptional quality allows us to measure the magnitude of this loss. A kiosk, called the White Chapel, was erected at Karnak by King Sesostris I for his jubilee (c. 1940 BC). This masterpiece was entirely reconstructed *(anastylosis)* fifty years ago by the French Egyptologist Henri Chevrier and is in almost perfect condition today.

Used as a repository for the sacred barque during religious ceremonies, the small open-sided raised kiosk, accessible by shallow axial ramps on each side, was built on a square plan with 16 white limestone pillars supporting a flat roof crowned by a cavetto cornice. The fine limestone walls and columns were admirably sculpted with reliefs of exceptional quality. Demolished in the Eighteenth Dynasty (New Kingdom), the fragments were used as rubble to fill the third pylon of the Karnak temple, where archeologists discovered them. Henri Chevrier was able to reconstruct the kiosk by a patient study of the texts and the scenes sculpted on the different pieces. Thus bringing back to life one of the most attractive architectural creations of the period. With its purity and refined simplicity, the White Chapel represents a perfect example of the work of the master-builders during the Middle Kingdom.

## The expansion of the Faiyum

The greatest accomplishment of the Middle Kingdom, however, lay in the rapid development of an uncultivated, semi-arid region of Egypt to the west of Lisht and Dahshur, the Faiyum depression, which was developed into a vast oasis. Thanks to the canalization of the Bahr Yussef branch of the Nile, these rich lands were carefully irrigated. Settlers were sent there to cultivate the desert around the marshes and the hippopotamus-and crocodile-infested waters of Lake Qarun. The Middle

Opposite:

**King Sesostris III: portrait of a disenchanted and bitter king who reigned over Lower Egypt around 1850 BC.**

The head, carved in pink granite, was found in the Temple of Amun at Karnak in 1970. It is one of the most striking examples of pharaonic statuary. Following the radiant and idealized portraits from the Old Kingdom, this Middle Kingdom sovereign displays human feelings. (Museum of Ancient Egyptian Art, Luxor)

**Scenes of Bedouins copied by Champollion from a Middle Kingdom rock tombs at Beni Hasan.**

The tomb of the nomarch Khnumhotep (1890 BC) dates from the reign of King Sesostris I. Here, Asiatic nomads of the Amu tribe are depicted with their donkey crossing the desert, transporting arms and baggage: bows and arrows, a club, and a "prophet's lyre," an instrument that the Egyptians did not adopt until the New Kingdom. These color reproductions were published in Paris in 1835.

Kingdom pharaohs organized an intense agricultural activity, providing the country with grain reserves and productive orchards.

It was in the Faiyum Oasis that King Amenemhet III built the Pyramid of Hawara flanked by a mortuary temple. This vast limestone complex was formed by a series of chapels with cambered roofs and must have constituted an impressive ensemble with its numerous passageways and outbuildings. Already a sightseeing attraction in the Greco-Roman era, the complexity of the plan and the ruinous state of the site understandably led Herodotus to mistake it for a labyrinth.

### The tombs of the Middle Kingdom

Sites such as Aswan, Beni Hasan, Asyut, and the Theban West Bank have yielded up many private tombs dating from the First Intermediary Period and from the Middle Kingdom. Those of the Twelfth Dynasty (*c.* 1990-1780 BC) hewn out of the rock of the western cliffs are characterized by hypostyle halls supported as often by square pillars as by proto-Doric columns.

In addition to the usual decorations of reliefs and texts, many clay statuettes and wooden maquettes of ships, houses, stores and even troops and servants accumulated in these tombs. These sculpted or painted pictorial representations were invaluable in expressing the needs of the deceased in afterlife. At once suggestive and touching in their naiveté, they help us understand the everyday life of the ancient Egyptians and give an idea of how they navigated on the Nile and on the Mediterranean Sea.

### The fortresses defending Egypt

During the Old Kingdom's first period of stability, no other strongholds were needed except to reinforce the military outposts along the defeated territories. The kings of the Middle Kingdom followed a policy of expansion and established settlements in Upper Nubia, and under Sesostris III a string of fortresses was erected along the southern borders.

The ancient Egyptians acquired an elaborate technology for the construction of fortifications and demonstrated an extraordinary mastery of the art of conducting and resisting sieges *(poliorcetics)* as early as the Predynastic Age before the Third Millennium. Towers, curtain walls, covered ways, and hidden doors built into the bastions allowed the

**Wall-painting from a tomb at Beni Hasan showing Bedouins trying to domesticate gazelles.**

Copied by Champollion from Khnumhotep's tomb (Twelfth Dynasty), the picture shows the nomads taming and fattening wild desert gazelles. The Amus were always represented with an abundant head of hair and a black beard. Their heavy wool clothing—in particular the colorful shepherd's cloak with a herringbone pattern—sets them apart from the Egyptians with their loincloths and light linen dresses.

**Semi-circular bastion of the Buhen fortress in Upper Nubia.**

From the Middle Kingdom on, Egypt fortified its southern borders. The city of Buhen along the Nile at the level of the second cataract, south of Abu Simbel, served as an important stronghold against invasion from the Nubians. At the time, the Egyptians had conceived an elaborate defense strategy as this architecture of thick mudbricks demonstrates. Behind a first set of bastion walls and a glacis, a curtain wall studded with square towers provided additional protection.

defenders to dominate their assailants on their flanks. The cuspated walls surrounding the Old Kingdom city of Memphis–which served as a model for King Djoser's funerary complex built by Imhotep at Saqqara–were actually fortifications. As we have already seen, the great master-builder had petrified an initial type of mudbrick construction dating back to the first unification of the Two Lands.

At Buhen, on the river bank near the second cataract, stood the ruins of an enormous stronghold which has since disappeared under the Aswan Dam lake. The square fortress comprised a glacis and a moat and spread over 6 acres (2½ hectares). Behind the outer curtain walls studded with semi-circular bastions, rose cuspated walls 33ft (10m) high and 16ft (5m) thick entirely made of mudbrick. Square towers were set out at regular intervals along the crenellated curtain walls and round towers had loopholes pierced at two different levels. Vestiges of corbels seem to indicate the presence of projecting parapets with openings in the floor *(machicolation)* through which projectiles could be dropped on the enemy.

### The invasion of the Hyksos

This line of defense demonstrates the care which the Egyptians took to stop any incursions into their territory by bands of Nubians. But the greatest threat was from marauders from the Northeast–where it was more difficult to protect the borders–who penetrated deeply into the Delta area at the end of the reign of Amenemhet III, around 1800 BC. Strengthened by steadily increasing immigration until their number was sufficiently great and the time ripe for a concerted push, these tribes seized Memphis and proclaimed rule of Lower Egypt. The Egyptian troops that held Byblos and Ugarit in Syria would now lose their eastern empire. This population of Palestinian origin, called the Hyksos, was eventually recognized as a new family of pharaohs and formed the Fifteenth and Sixteenth Dynasties of the list compiled by Manetho, a learned high priest of Heliopolis commissioned by Ptolemy I in the 3rd century BC to write a history of Egypt. Modern historians still make judicious use of this comprehensive list of kings and accept his numbering of dynasties.

After the Hyksos claimed Lower Egypt from their capital at Avaris, the country fell into a period of decadence that lasted until about 1660 BC. Once again, following the golden age of the Middle Kingdom with its sumptuous treasures discovered at Illahun and Dahshur, Egypt

**The double line of fortification of the Buhen fortress along the Nile.**

This Egyptian stronghold, forty centuries old, attests to the elaborate techniques of Pharaonic fortifications. The high towers and monumental gateways served to control troop movements on the river as well as on the banks of the Nile. All the structures had long ago fallen into ruin when this photograph was taken in 1960. Today the whole site has disappeared under the lake formed by the Aswan Dam.

entered into another phase of regression and turmoil. This was to be called the Second Intermediary Period. Yet, while the northern regions were plunged in strife in the hands of barbarians, another renewal began to gather momentum in Upper Egypt. A line of vassal princes from Thebes, forming the Seventeenth Dynasty (*c.* 1650-1550 BC), eventually felt themselves strong enough to challenge the Hyksos usurpers and overthrow them. They reunited Egypt and Nubia and thus ensured the survival of the Two Lands.

Left and opposite:

**Wooden models discovered in the Necropolis of the Asyut princes.**

The Italian Egyptologist Schiaparelli discovered these small figures and boats of sculpted wood in the tomb of a Middle Kingdom dignitary named Shemes at a site south of Tell el-Amarna. The oarsmen face the coxswain who is setting the pace, while at the stern a standing vigil checks the depth. (Museo Egizio, Turin)

# ASCENDANCY
## OF UPPER EGYPT

### THE BLOOM
### OF NEW-KINGDOM ART

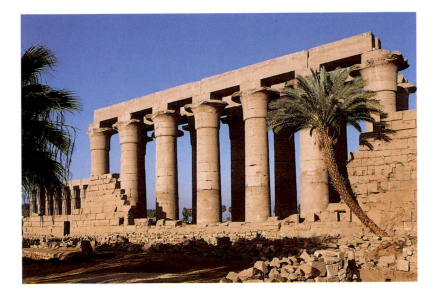

*The large alley of King Amenophis III at the Amun-Re Temple of Luxor with its bell-shaped capitals.*

Following the chaos provoked by the Hyksos take-over in the Nile Delta at the threshold of the New Kingdom, what type of architecture would the Egyptian master-builders produce? This was an important question for a civilization steeped in tradition and respectful of the past, for it was in fact architecture that provided the frame-work for spiritual observances.

No matter what technical innovations were adopted by the architects, their work was always based on a legacy handed down by previous builders. The New Kingdom inherited a stock of knowledge that would be developed in new directions, with changes in style however that never totally broke with the past. Early monuments of the New Kingdom perpetuated a continuity with those of the

Opposite:

**The west colonnade bordering the Amenophis III courtyard in the temple of Amun-Re at Luxor.**

Built around 1400 BC, the row of fasciculated papyrus columns still supporting an entablature possesses an lightness that is unique in pharaonic architecture. Several undamaged statues recently dug up in the middle of the courtyard and dating from the New Kingdom were buried there for protection against invaders.

**The Kiosk of King Amenophis I in Karnak reconstructed by archeologists.**

The blocks of this repository chapel, used as rubble to fill up the core of the third pylon of the Temple of Amun, were found along with those of the Kiosk of Sesostris. Archeologists have carefully reconstructed the edifice (*anastylosis*) which served to house the sacred barque during the ritual jubilee processions. The simple style of this Eighteenth Dynasty monument (c. 1550 BC), with angles bordered by torus moldings and crowned by a cavetto cornice, was inherited from the Middle Kingdom.

Opposite:

**The granite obelisk erected by King Tuthmosis I at the entrance of the fourth pylon at Karnak.**

This stone needle, 75 ft (23 m) high and weighing about 160 tons, was erected around 1530 BC in front of the first of the Karnak temples of the Middle Kingdom.

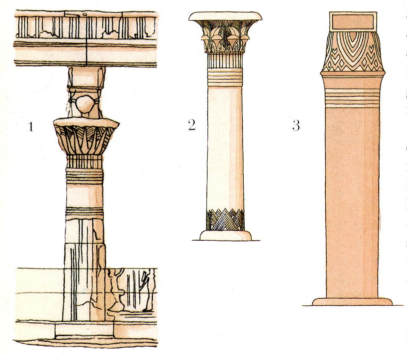

1. Hathoric column,
2. column with a composite bell-shaped capital,
3. tentpole column.

Middle Kingdom. King Amenophis I's Chapel of the Barque (*c.* 1550 BC), for example, possessed a simplicity and elegance that evoked another masterpiece built 400 years earlier–King Sesostris I's White Chapel (*c.* 1940 BC).

In the middle of the Second Millennium BC, Egyptian architects had already acquired a wide inventory of forms and modes of expression. As early as the Third Dynasty, they were using fluted columns and composite capitals sculpted with leaf motifs. In the Fourth Dynasty they produced square granite pillars. During the Fifth Dynasty, they added cylindrical supports (Sahure Temple at Abusir), palm capitals (Temple of the Userkaf Pyramid at Saqqara), and papyrus capitals on fasciculated columns imitating bundled reeds or plant stems (High Temple of Niuserre at Abu Ghurab). In the Middle Kingdom they created superb polygonal shafts with eight, twelve or sixteen sides. Indeed, the master-builders could chose from a varied and original repertory of forms, volumes and designs. Among the hundreds of temples built in Egypt no two are exactly alike, no more than two identical Romanesque or Gothic churches could be found.

## Thebes

Thebes, now called Luxor, one of the greatest cities of antiquity, lay 300 miles (500km) due south of Memphis and was developed in the midst of an ideal environment at the confluence of the gorges of Wadi Hammamat which form one of the few natural links with the Red Sea. These gorges, between the Libyan and Arabian mountain ranges, were graced with exceptionally fertile land.

No trace remains of the places of worship built in the cities of the Old Kingdom. Unlike Thebes, neither Memphis nor Heliopolis have preserved the ruins of any noteworthy buildings. Thebes has preserved not only funerary shrines, but also vestiges of temples devoted to the great Egyptian divinities such as Amun, the sun-god for whom the priests set up an endowment dating back to the Middle Kingdom (Temple of Karnak), and Amun-Re, who was worshipped during the solemn processions of the Feast of Opet (Temple of Luxor).

With the dawn of the Middle Kingdom, the Western Bank of the Nile saw the decline of the great pyramids offset by the considerable development of funerary temples. The architectural efforts of the pharaohs were now spent on royal sanctuaries independent of the tomb sites. There was very little difference however between

**The Mortuary Temple of Queen Hatshepsut beneath the high cliffs of Deir el-Bahri.**

The architect Senenmut, favorite of Queen Hatshepsut, built this funerary edifice around 1490 BC on a scale larger than the nearby monument erected for King Mentuhotep II, whose ruins with ramp and terrace still intact, can be seen in the background. Surrounded by rock at the foot of the Theban hills, the three levels of the sanctuary's broad terraces are remarkable for their modernity. The third level underwent major restoration work during the 1970s.

**Proto-Doric columns of the Anubis chapel north of the Hatshepsut Temple.**

These sixteen-sided columns with a simple abacus serving as capital form a hypostyle hall bearing twelve shafts. Inside, the wall-paintings have preserved their colors and the roof slabs are carved with stars on a blue background. The door to the right leads into a small chapel devoted to Anubis, the dog-headed god of embalming, often associated with Osiris, god of resurrection.

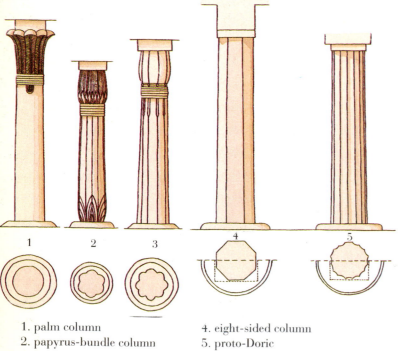

1. palm column
2. papyrus-bundle column
3. lotus column
4. eight-sided column
5. proto-Doric
   or sixteen-sided column

temples dedicated to gods and funerary temples dedicated to kings, for both of these were representations of Creation and the Cosmos. Their design reflected the universe and manifested order emerging from primeval chaos.

In cult temples, the local god was regarded by the community as a living entity actually present and in residence. The clergy of each temple was entrusted with a spiritual mission and took on the responsibility of the rituals that were performed within its walls. Its purpose was to capture cosmic energy in order to put it to good use and to conjure particular supernatural powers to help keep the wheel of life in motion. The results were supposed to benefit the local population who received the divine word, as well as the pharaoh who thus acquired the force to rule from his temple-palace, and then gain everlasting life in the manner of the gods. The privilege of immortality which the kings began to share with their retinue as early as the Fourth Dynasty, was more and more widely distributed during the New Empire.

### Rebirth from the south

Lower Egypt, from the Delta to the city of Memphis, had twice been through times of trouble and decline, and each time, salvation came from Upper Egypt, where a certain isolation allowed the Egyptian sovereigns to re-establish their authority.

As we have already seen, at the end of the Old Kingdom the country entered a time of civil unrest known as the First Intermediate Period, which ended two centuries later with the emergence of the Mentuhotep kings of Thebes (Eleventh Dynasty), who successfully challenged the foreign rulers of Heracleopolis and brought about the re-unification of the Two Lands. The ascension of this dynasty to the throne revived the prestige of the Southern Kingdom, but the pharaohs returned once again to Memphis in the Twelfth Dynasty, restoring Lower Egypt to its traditional position of supremacy.

The collapse of the Thirteenth Dynasty heralded the end of the Middle Kingdom and the beginning of the Second Intermediate Period, which was marked by the Hyksos occupation of the Delta. After a second period of disorder, Upper Egypt experienced another moment of glory (c. 1550 BC) which turned Thebes—the "City of a Hundred Doors" described in ancient Greek texts—into the capital of an empire whose influence would spread

over the entire Near East. The expulsion of the Hyksos by the Thebans marked the beginning of the New Kingdom and the relocation of the capital back at Thebes. Despite a series of crises that would have destroyed weaker monarchs, Egypt then enjoyed a golden age of art and architecture.

## The rise of the New Kingdom

Thus Nationalistic fervor was awakened in the southern provinces. King Kamosis, the last Theban pharaoh of the Seventeenth Dynasty, was the instigator of this pan-Egyptian renaissance. He defeated the Hyksos rulers and recaptured Memphis. His brother Ahmose, having won the siege of Avaris (c. 1580 BC), reunited Egypt and Nubia and became the first sovereign of the New Kingdom, a time which saw Egypt rise to unparalleled prosperity. Ahmose's son Amenophis I began a reconstruction campaign and renewal of activity throughout the country with the re-organizing of agriculture, the re-introducing of irrigation and the reviving of international trade. Under the reigns of Tuthmosis I and Tuthmosis II, Egypt entered a phase of expansion lasting for nearly 500 years which was characterized by pharaonic control over Egypt, as well as Palestine and Syria. For art historians this period represents the age which left the most documentary sources and the greatest number of art objects, including numerous inscriptions and admirable reliefs, paintings, and statuary many of which are in an excellent state of conservation. It ended with the onset of the Amarnian crisis, when the schismatic King Amenophis IV–known as Akhenaten–brought the Eighteenth Dynasty to a halt.

Dynastic unrest arose at the death of Tuthmosis II, who was the first husband of Queen Hatshepsut. Still in her youth, she married her stepson and nephew Tuthmosis III, but kept him away from the throne, exercising the royal power herself in conjunction with her vizier, the architect Senenmut. She reigned like a pharaoh and was often represented with a ceremonial beard and wearing the Double Crown (pschent).

Tired of attending to military campaigns on the eastern borders, Queen Hatshepsut devoted herself to great architectural projects from 1504 until 1483 BC. The first major effort to stimulate new artistic activity was the construction of her funerary temple at Deir el-Bahri on a site already dominated by the earlier monument devoted to King Mentuhotep II. During these years, the humiliated

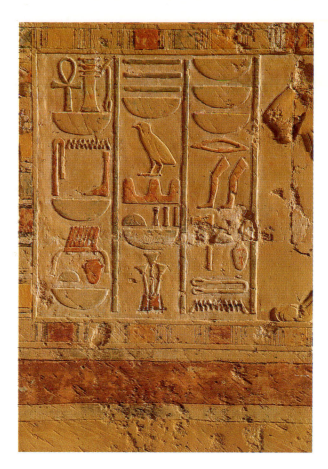

**Detail of a polychrome inscription in the Temple of Hatshepsut at Deir el-Bahri.**

The hieroglyphs are carved in raised relief and touched up with warm colors.

Opposite:

**Colossal granite statue of Queen Hatshepsut.**

The Queen wears the pharaonic insignia: *nemes*, *uraeus*, and a ceremonial beard. Nonetheless, her features are feminine in this portrait that King Tuthmosis III appropriated after his much-hated aunt's death. (Egyptian Museum, Cairo)

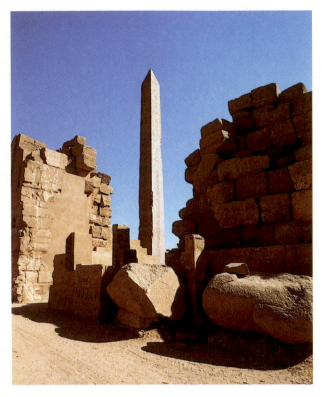

**The Obelisk of Queen Hatshepsut.**

Of the two obelisks that were placed by the Queen at the entrance of the ancient Temple of Karnak, only one is still standing. It stands 100ft (30m) high and weighs 700 tons. Below. Perfectly carved hieroglyphs at the bottom of the Queen's obelisk.

Tuthmosis III could only wait for his aunt's death before finally ascending to the throne and taking his revenge.

## The Temple of Queen Hatshepsut

Queen Hatshepsut's temple at Deir el-Bahri, built under the direction of Senenmut (*c.* 1490 BC), drew its inspiration from the earlier nearby Mentuhotep monument, raised almost 500 years earlier, but surpassed it in lightness and spaciousness. However, there was no real break with the past and the queen's temple can not be considered an innovation in comparison with the older model. In both complexes, the most striking features were the human-scale proportions and the plainness of the architectural treatment. This trend in Egyptian art broke with the gigantism of the Old Kingdom, yet differed from the immense creations of the Ramessides that would be built in the next centuries. The Queen adopted the same architectural options as those of her precursor: causeways and inclined ramps connecting series of terraces fronted by porticos with double rows of pillars leading to sanctuaries cut into the hills behind *(hypogea).*

The bold contrast between the broad flat man-made constructions and the splendor of Western Thebes' limestone hills towering above is remarkable. At this spot the curving sweep of the cliffs presents steep vertical rifts rising like great organ pipes, a grandeur to which the majestic spread of the monument below responds. Dominating this grandiose setting, the "Peak of the West," rising with the symbolic mass of a pyramid, offered the sovereigns their final place of rest. In time, other *hypogea* were hewn out of the cliff higher up, closer to its emblematic summit. The modern reconstruction of the temple started at the turn of this century and continues to this day; the third level is being rebuilt under the direction of the Polish Archeological Institute.

## Gardens and Terraces

Situated at the edge of the arable land, the area around the queen's temple formed a panorama of nature, from marshlands to changeless rocks of the desert, from fragile seasons of growth to hostile mineral wastelands. A three-quarter mile-long (1km) forecourt with gardens formed a link between the landscape and the architecture. On one side, a pool planted with papyrus evoked the primitive valley; the other side was lined with incense-bearing trees suggesting a mythical and sacred shrine. Farther along, an

**The two granite pillars raised by King Tuthmosis III in the center of the Amun temple in Karnak.**

These pillars symbolize Upper and Lower Egypt with the papyrus and the lotus and are placed on the reverse side of the sixth pylon in front of the kiosk of the sacred barque.

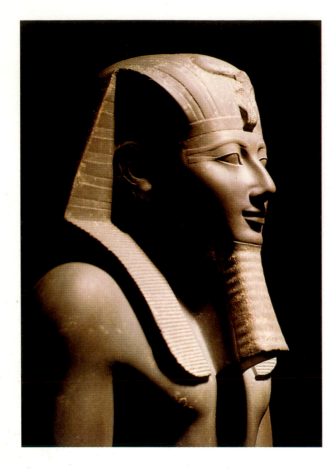

**Idealized portrait of King Tuthmosis III sculpted in schist.**

Queen Hatshepsut's nephew represented with all the appointments of a sovereign. His aquiline profile, gentle smile and eyes lengthened with make-up give him an expression of eternal contentment and triumph. (Museum of Ancient Egyptian Art, Luxor)

alley lined with stone sphinxes led up to a gateway—no longer in existence—that opened into a mudbrick enclosure.

From here, terraces rose up level by level to the foot of the cliff over a distance of 800ft (240m). On either side of the two flights of ramps, platforms extended in front of symmetrical porticos, flanked by two rows of eleven pillars. The middle terrace consisted of a colonnade of square pillars with a south chapel dedicated to Hathor with Hathoric capitals, and one devoted to Anubis on the north with fluted polygonal columns. The colonnade of the upper terrace was supported by colossal Osiride pillars representing Queen Hatshepsut. Beyond a granite gateway lay a peristyle court surrounded by fluted polygonal columns leading into a complex dominated by an open courtyard with an altar for the worship of the sun god. The shrine itself was cut into the cliff behind. All the walls and porticos were decorated with magnificent sunk reliefs relating the exploits of the reign, such as the expedition to the Land of Punt. The Hathor chapel, which once housed the statue of the sacred cow, has preserved its blue star-covered vault.

Ancient Egypt contributed few monuments as strong yet as harmonious and pure as the temple of Queen Hatshepsut. This did not prevent Tuthmosis III, however, from taking revenge after the Queen's death: the reliefs were defaced, her cartouches excised, and all the representations of the Queen and her vizier were consigned to oblivion.

In later times on the same site at Deir el-Bahri, Senenmut was associated with a cult devoted to the great pharaonic architects Imhotep and Amenhotep-son-of-Hapu; the three great master-builders were deified and worshipped as healing gods.

The temple of the Queen must have served as an incentive to her successor. In 1962, Polish archeologists discovered a shrine that King Tuthmosis III had erected on a natural terrace dominating the monuments of King Mentuhotep and Queen Hatshepsut. It was composed essentially of a hypostyle hall with chapels hewn out of the cliff, and reached by a long ramp. Painted reliefs and many fine statues were found on this site.

### The Temples of Amun at Karnak and Luxor (Thebes)

The Eighteenth Dynasty embarked on enormous building projects of temples devoted to the highly venerated god Amun-Re, in Karnak as well as Luxor. The

**Feast hall built by Tuthmosis III at Karnak.**

Beyond the Middle Kingdom sanctuary (no longer existing) that formed the ancient Great Temple of Amun, this basilical construction with five naves set crosswise to a central axis is a hypostyle erected around 1480 BC. It measures 141 ft (44 m) long and contains twenty columns bordering a raised central aisle, and 32 exterior pillars. This is where the jubilee ceremonies took place.

**Amun represented on a polychrome relief at the funerary temple of King Tuthmosis III.**

Discovered in 1962 among the ruins of a temple that the King dedicated to himself and to the great Theban god at Deir el-Bahri. This superb detail shows the divinity Amun-Min wearing the double-feathered headdress, the ceremonial beard and a large polychrome necklace. (Museum of Ancient Egyptian Art, Luxor)

layout of the gigantic sanctuary in Karnak was so complex and the ruins in such a fragmented state that it has been almost impossible to reconstitute the history of the monument which went through a series of building campaigns that spanned more than fifteen centuries.

King Tuthmosis III ordered a vast enclosure and two pylons to be raised around a courtyard that dated back to the Middle Kingdom. These enormous trapezoidal masses framing the entranceway were a great architectural innovation, even if buildings from the Twelfth Dynasty (Qâoun el-Kebir near Asyut, and the façade of Kasr el-Sâgha at Faiyum) were forerunners. Their shape symbolized the hill behind which the sun rose. They were characterized by battered walls similar to primitive constructions (mastabas) surmounted by cavetto cornices and torus moldings that evoked the ancient mudbrick architecture that was reinforced by straw padding.

Around 1500 BC, Queen Hatshepsut added a pair of obelisks on each side of the already existing temple. The highest obelisk measured 100ft (30m). These 700-ton monoliths were brought down from Aswan and required the construction of a gigantic wooden boat. The extraordinary feat of engineering required to raise the stone needles was narrated in the scenes sculpted on the walls of a red granite chapel that has since been reconstructed from the rubble fragments also found inside one of the pylons in Karnak.

It was King Tuthmosis III who undertook the basic additions to the temple during the Eighteenth Dynasty. He had a limestone hypostyle hall built with five naves, called the Hall of the Feasts, which was supported by strange columns that have been described as "tent poles," narrower at the base than at the top (this was perhaps influenced by Minoan architecture, the Knossos Palace dates from the same period).

Then King Amenophis III (*c.* 1400 BC), an able politician as well as a tireless builder, erected a great 360ft wide (110 m) pylon in front of the whole temple complex against which the vast hypostyle hall of Sethos I and Ramesses II would later be built. Amenophis III also added two obelisks at the rear.

This same ruler was responsible for most of the Luxor temple including the great processional colonnade supported by 14 immense, smooth-sided columns with bell-shaped capitals rising to 52ft (16m), the elegant peristyled courtyard with papyrus-bundled columns, and many chapels. All these constructions attest to the

92

**The alley of the sphinxes symbolizing Amun at the Great Temple at Karnak.**

At the beginning of the Eighteenth Dynasty the local Theban divinity became dominant. An alley leading from the temple to a pier on the Nile is bordered with statues of the god Amun, represented with the body of a lion and the head of a ram (criosphinx).

skill of Amenhotep-son-of-Hapu the architect of King Amenophis III, who built other monuments including the Amenophium, a colossal temple in Western Thebes. This last complex, spread out over an area of 6,500 square feet (600 square meters) in a fertile valley, was built of mudbrick adorned with decorations in stucco and sandstone. Nothing is left of this building today, except for the two Colossi of Memnon–representations of the sovereign seated on his throne in front of the compound's majestic entrance. These quartzite monoliths (the one on the right was restored in Antiquity) are 66ft (20m) high and weigh several hundred tons.

The use of a mudbrick technique for this funerary temple, as was also the case for the temple that Amenhotep-son-of-Hapu constructed nearby, is surprising in that it contradicts the principles already adopted by the Egyptian architects to ensure an everlasting permanence to the royal sanctuaries. This choice may have resulted from the fact that the monuments stood on fertile soil and not on solid rock. But even more astounding was the use of brick arches for the roofs of the chambers. It was most likely these unusual techniques–particularly the invention of a true arch–that elevated Amenhotep-son-of-Hapu to the status of a god.

Thus in the region of Thebes, the master-builders of the Eighteenth Dynasty accomplished a sizable number of monuments of major importance during the first phase of the New Empire.

**Detail of a sphinx with the head of King Amenophis III.**

Sculpted in sandstone, the head incarnates the King represented as Atum, the sun god; it was found at Karnak. (Museo Egizio, Turin)

Opposite:

**The famous Colossi of Memnon representing King Amenophis III on his throne.**

Behind these gigantic sculptures once rose the immense funerary temple of King Amenophis III, built in brick by the architect Amenhotep-son-of-Hapu. Of the two statues, the one in the foreground has retained its monolithic character and rests on a base solidly anchored in the silt. The second, restored in antiquity with square stone blocks, is today in a state of ruin. Figures of two queens stand at each side of the king's legs: Mutemonia is the mother of the sovereign, the other, Tiye, was his wife.

# THE TOMB
## A GLORIFICATION OF LIFE

*A charming and youthful profile of a woman evokes nothing death-like. In Egypt, plebeian tombs glorified the bliss of life on earth.*

**Portrait from the tomb of Maya at Deir el-Medina.**

These Eighteenth Dynasty paintings in tempera were removed from a tomb by Schiaparelli and transported to the Turin Museum in 1905. The two figures sitting on elegant chairs are parents of the scribe and artist Maya. (Museo Egizio, Turin)

Little remains of the domestic architecture from the cities and villages of Ancient Egypt except for a few insignificant ruins. Built for the most part of battered mudbrick walls with terraced roofs supported by palm logs and adjoined by thatched lean-tos, none of the peasant, craftsman or noble dwellings have survived the passage of time, floods and fire. Only rare cities built on the edge of deserts and then abandoned (Deir el-Medina or Tell el-Amarna) have remained sufficiently undamaged to reveal some of their secrets.

From the Third Dynasty onward, a desire for more permanent religious monuments led the Egyptians to adopt stone and rock-hewn constructions. We have been able to grasp a better understanding of the Egyptians' art of building by reconstructing or studying the stone vestiges of funerary monuments such as the temples–houses dedicated to gods–and tombs–repositories of the dead.

## Beliefs about Eternal Life

According to Egyptian mythology, the creative and preserving power of life, the *ka*, was inherent in every being and accompanied them, like a kind of double, until their death. The *ka* lived on, but left its mortal home and returned to its divine origin. This spiritual personality whether belonging to a god or a human required the same care if it were to survive eternally. The Egyptians believed that the gods had been born and had lived for thousands of years before man, but that like humans, they had died and been buried. Some of the temples built in their honor also represented their burial sites. The god's *ka* was summoned to the cult temple through an effigy in the form of a statue or sometimes a painted portrait.

The function of the high priest was to provide for the needs of the gods. Upon entering the temple each morning with offerings, the priest would carefully remove the cloth wrapped around the gold or silver statue and clean it with water and natron (salt). He would then apply eye makeup to the god's face and wrap it up again it in layers of clean linen while chanting the appropriate prayers.

To further content the divinity, the effigy underwent ritual fumigations, was entreated with chants and hymns and exhibited in processions before being replaced in its tabernacle *(naos)*. As with the gods, a mortuary chapel was devoted to the cult the *ka* of a dead man, whether king or wealthy commoner. Tomb owners created endowments to perpetuate their own memory and that of their ancestors and provided funds for the construction of monuments and the carrying out of rituals.

## Mummification

A complex theology reconciled the different traditions of Ancient Egypt with regard to the destiny of the dead during their afterlife. The concepts expressed in the sacred texts carved on the walls and written on rolls of papyrus deposited in the sepulchers are far from uniform. One thing is certain, though, and that is that their belief in resurrection required the conservation of the body. From this belief evolved the embalming techniques that

**Reproduced by Ippolito Rosellini around 1820, this scene shows
Anubis, the jackal-headed god of the dead, tending a mummy.**

Before being placed in a sarcophagus, the deceased was laid out on a bed
decorated with lion heads. Represented under the funerary couch are the
four canopic vases with the heads of Horus' four sons: a falcon, a jackal,
a baboon, and a human. On either side the protecting goddesses Isis and
Nephthys preside over the embalming.

**Anubis proceeds to embalm a deceased in a pyramid-shaped tabernacle.**

A bird-soul with a human head escapes from the dead body. The Theban wall-painting reproduced by Rosellini represents the deceased's parents in ceremonial costumes bearing offerings, seated at the foot of a fig tree laden with fruit. A rustic divinity in the tree provides food for the dead.

100

**The deceased's last voyage in a barque.**

Inside his sarcophagus protected by a light canopy, the deceased is being transported by sacred barque across the Nile, which also represented the river of the Great Beyond. A priest accompanies the mummy and a cantor is reciting the traditional litanies. Professional mourners precede the chest containing canopic vases which is carried on a handbarrow with the god Anubis. They cry out lamentations and throw dust on their heads. Below, the heavy casket encased in a gilt tabernacle rests on a barque, itself placed on a sledge pulled by four oxen. A priest scatters incense over the catafalque. These copies were made by Rosellini around 1820.

**The offering-table replete with food for the afterlife.**

A tray with a haunch of veal, a calf's head, a goose, and colored baskets filled with fruits are presented on a silver stand in the form of a tapered pillar. On the ground, a tripod holds a recipient for beverages. Rosellini isolated this detail from a larger painting depicting offerings to the dead.

accompanied complicated funerary rituals.

The Egyptians were so obsessed with survival after death that they developed an elaborate art of mummification derived from the natural desiccation of cadavers that took place in early pit burials. After cleaning and evisceration, the body was dried in the sand. The brain and internal organs–heart, lungs, liver, and intestines–were handled separately and placed in special vessels known as canopic jars. The body was then washed with palm wine and placed in natron for seventy days to allow it to completely dry out. This process brought about a discoloration of the hair giving rise to speculations about a blond or redheaded population.

Every part of the corpse was then enveloped in fine linen; each limb, each finger, was wrapped in yards of bandages until the mummy, with talismans and amulets applied to precise areas of the body during the different stages of the process, came to look like a swaddled infant. Anointing perfumes and oils completed these preparations during which a priest recited endless prayers and incantations assimilating the deceased with Osiris, the great god of the dead who had come back to life.

On the day of the funeral a priest performed a special ceremony called the Opening of the Mouth, when ritual instruments were laid on the mummy's head to restore breath and speech. The funeral ceremony took place before the image of the deceased with incense burning and recitations of spells, conferring on him the strength to leave his terrestrial grave and resuscitate in the Other World.

### The writings of the magic ritual

During the Old Kingdom the funerary ceremonies held by the priests were accompanied by litanies from texts that dated back to prehistory. Many magic spells from the *Pyramid Texts* were assimilated later on into the *Coffin Texts* painted onto the wooden coffins of the Middle Kingdom. At the time of the New Kingdom a collection of passages from the *Book of the Dead* accompanied the deceased kings or nobles to the tomb. These sacred formulae were available to a larger elite and this resulted in a certain democratization of the cult. The main themes, with variations, treated the existence of the deceased in the afterlife.

Another text known as the *Book of What is in the Underworld* described this netherland and indicated the

**The Weighing of the Heart (*psychostasis*) on a papyrus sheet from
the *Book of the Dead*.**

The jackal-headed god Anubis weighs the heart of the deceased on the
scales of judgment. For the Egyptians, the heart is the resting-place of
the soul, and the weight of its sins must not exceed that of the Feather of
Truth worn by Maat, goddess of Justice. (Museo Egizio, Turin)

**During the New Kingdom, versions of the *Book of the Dead* were placed with the deceased in their tombs.**

This superb scene painted on a papyrus sheet depicts the heart being weighed in the presence of Osiris, according to chapter 125 of the Sacred Book: the god of the Dead and of Resurrection is seated in his shrine (*naos*) in a columned sanctuary surmounted by a cavetto cornice. Present at the ceremony are Maat, wearing his emblematic feather and Thoth, the ibis-headed god, scribe of the psychostasia, as well as Seth, the hippopotamus of the marshes. The divine judge must open the doors of the Great Beyond and introduce the deceased to a happy afterlife.
(Museo Egizio, Turin)

path followed by Re, the sun god, in his solar barque. In the Valley of the Kings, walls of tombs were covered with potent spells helping the deceased overcome the most dire adversity. The *Book of the Caverns* guided the tomb owners past the guardians of the Gates of the Twelve Hours of the Night along his route and helped him reach enlightenment. All these symbolic writings, distant versions of the religious traditions adopted a thousand years earlier, also transmitted the precepts that directed the embalming procedures. They contained astronomical information and even provided a chart of the Other World and descriptions of the monsters that inhabited it. They disclosed the different phases of the Weighing of the Heart *(psychostasia)*, a ceremonial presided by Osiris in which the heart of the deceased was weighed on a scale by Anubis, the keeper of the scales, and the heart had to be as light as an ostrich feather.

### Structure of the tomb

In the earliest times, only the king could attain eternal life inside his magnificent sepulcher thanks to an elaborate process of deification. He was then believed to ascend to the underside of the solar system to join the everlasting celestial bodies and sail across the firmament. The Sovereign Lord of the Two Lands became one with the sun god and "sat on the right hand of Re among the heavens." *(Text of the Pyramids)*. It was believed that the sun set in the world of the living, but rose in the underworld. Thus the West became the site of royal cemeteries where the tombs of nobles and courtiers were clustered around those of the divine master whom they hoped to join in the Other World. During the New Kingdom, the tombs of the nobles were planned out in the same fashion as those of the sovereigns.

The tomb itself was usually composed of two distinct parts: chapel and crypt. The highly decorated vestibule of the funerary chapel accommodated a false door—the symbol linking the living with the dead—and a carved image of the tomb owner. This hall was flanked by several smaller rooms housing the deceased's provisions such as victuals, furniture, offerings, sacred texts, etc.

To the rear, a burial shaft below ground led to the actual crypt. Although it was walled in or dissimulated by all sorts of subterfuges—pits, snares, booby traps, and false galleries—the storerooms and the chapel devoted to the cult remained accessible to the deceased's family and friends and to the priests who continued to perform

**The ushabti: indispensable mummyform figurines placed in the tomb.**

These statuettes representing servants or slaves were the so-called "answerers" who would carry out the necessary tasks in the next world. They could be counted by the hundreds in certain tombs. Most of the ushabtis were in pottery with a frit glaze or blue-green faience. (Musée du Louvre, Paris)

Opposite:

**At Deir el-Medina, a small pyramid indicates a tomb site.**

Perpetuating the ancient pyramid shape but constructed in miniature and built of brick and mud, sepulchers with exterior chapels surmount funerary vaults. In Upper Egypt these structures corresponded to the mastabas of the Old Kingdom near Memphis. A well leads from the chapel into a crypt, often decorated with scenes of offerings.

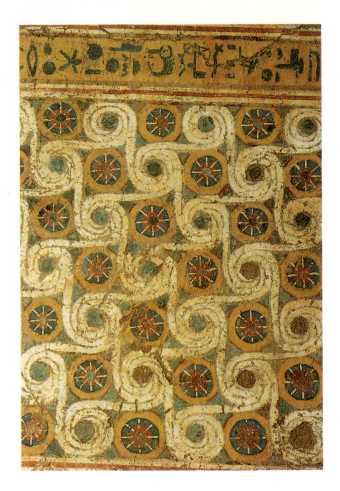

Above and opposite:

**The play of colors and forms on the ceiling of the Maya tomb.**

This sepulcher from Deir el-Medina, reconstituted at the Egyptian Museum of Turin in 1905, bears witness to Eighteenth-Dynasty popular art with abstract motifs of unequaled exuberance and spontaneity. The spirals evoke patterns from the Minoan civilization of Crete. The zigzags are reminiscent of weaving techniques, and the masterful rhythms and combinations of warm tones make a very decorative background for funerary art. (Museo Egizio, Turin)

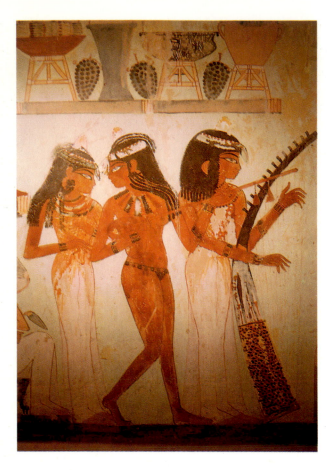

**The famous representation of dancers from the tomb of Nakht, the scribe of the Amun temple.**

This tomb at Sheikh abd el-Qurna (Western Thebes) facing Karnak dates from around 1425 BC. Painted on the walls of the sepulcher, young girls with a lute and harp animate the private banquets of the deceased.

rituals. The crypt was abundantly decorated with carved reliefs and wall paintings describing the truths expected to exist for eternity and depicting the figures of priests and servants who would accompany the deceased and his retinue to his afterlife.

The mummy was surrounded with all the necessary treasures, food, drink, clothing, and other essentials for sustenance in the next life, as well as small wooden models and *ushabtis* of terra cotta, frit glaze, or copper. These small statues were meant to carry out the tasks in the next world that the deceased might be called upon to do.

## Architecture of the tombs

In Upper Egypt as early as the Middle Kingdom, because of their dual function–chapel and crypt–tombs were composed of elements at the surface as well as underground. More-or-less massive above-ground stone constructions–mastabas or hypostyle halls–preceded the actual funerary temple. These were distinct from the subterranean structures and burial shafts leading down to the crypt. This resulted in a new architectural technique of cutting chambers directly out of the cliff face *(hypogea)*. During the New Kingdom, the actual burial sites, were carefully hidden in the Valley of the Kings to separate them from the funerary temples built on the edge of the Nile; this separation modified the traditional set up and permitted the temples to reach a considerable size without attracting attention to the graves themselves.

The Valley of the Kings is dominated by a natural pyramid called the Lady of the Peak. Here, tunnel-shaped rock-hewn passages, called *syrinx* by the Greeks, were excavated by specialized tomb builders. These craftsmen who lived in Deir el-Medina in Western Thebes have become very familiar to us, for archeologists discovered the ruins of their village and have been able to piece their lives together by deciphering the drawings and inscriptions on fragments of pottery *(ostracon)* found at the site.

Thanks to these remains, we have learned that this group of engineers and artists–sculptors, painters, scribes–were insubordinate at times; they organized the first strikes in history because their salary–paid in kind rather than in cash (fruit, vegetables, wine, drinking water, clothing, and tools)–was late in arriving from the royal palace. They did not hesitate to address themselves

**The deceased, gazing towards the heavens, awaits to be reborn in the afterlife.**

Simple mortals did not possess sarcophagi of gold, silver, nor even of granite. They were laid in an anthropomorphic case made of a painted and decorated cartonage of papyrus, a procedure which gave an expression of life to the deceased. This example from the Eighteenth or Nineteenth Dynasty is adorned with representations of the protective wings of Nut, goddess of the sky.

111

directly to the king, threatening to stop work on the royal tombs; having become indispensable, they obtained satisfaction.

These men worked like miners inside the hill, cutting layers of limestone and beds of silex to a depth of 500 ft (150 m). They hollowed out entire complexes of galleries, halls, storerooms, and chapels connected to each other by wells, false entrances, stairs, hypostyle halls and corridors. Under the direction of priests, artists adorned the walls with scenes from the *Book of the Dead* and painted immense frescos of funerary rituals which unraveled along the walls like papyrus scrolls.

These intrepid and indefatigable craftsmen became highly-skilled masters of color and line, a talent all the more remarkable when we take into account the difficulties under which they were forced to exercise their art. The Valley of the Kings and the Valley of the Queens are situated in a torrid world of rock where there is not the slightest trace of humidity. The workmen toiling in the depths lacked oxygen and had no light other than that of inadequate oil lamps (the present-day guides' tale of mirrors used by the ancient Egyptians is not plausible). This did not prevent the workers from extracting thousands of tons of rubble while craftsmen fashioned complex spaces, and artists covered thousands of square feet with scenes depicting an unreal world of gods, monsters, serpents and crocodiles, starry skies and terrifying oceans, called "that which exists in Hell."

### Art in the tombs of the nobles

The treasures stored in royal *hypogea*, of which the most fabulous belonged to a minor pharaoh King Tutankhamun, and the superb works of art reserved for the funerary decoration of the sovereigns do not convey the same kind of information as the tombs of the nobles who were more directly concerned with mundane occupations. Although they epitomize the worldly aspirations of the upper classes, they offer greater insight into Egyptian civilization as a whole. Their brightly colored walls are adorned with graceful scenes of workers, harvesters, grapepickers, and hunters, alongside scribes taking inventory of the treasures. A retinue of wailing mourners surrounded the deceased, but these sad and grieving figures were soon followed by scenes of lavish offerings piled up on funerary banquet tables among musicians and dancers seemingly full of life.

Above opposite

**The village of Deir el-Medina in a desert hollow on the border of the cultivated valley.**

A careful excavation of the site where the workmen of the necropolis lived shows traces of streets and houses belonging to the artists and artisans who worked at the Valley of the Kings and the Valley of the Queens. The foundations of these constructions made of rubble and dried mud revealed not only the layout of a city organized along a principal axis but give considerable insight into everyday life. The laborers built their own tombs around the city, often decorating them with taste and a touching naiveté.

Below opposite:

**The Hill of the West dominating the Valley of the Kings resembles a natural pyramid.**

The sovereigns of the New Kingdom were buried at the far end of this extremely arid hollow. Archeologists have counted sixty-one tombs hewn in the rock (*hypogea*) up to depths of 400ft (125m). Some are very simple, others more elaborate with vast subterranean apartments. Their entrances were hidden from grave robbers under piles of fallen rock.

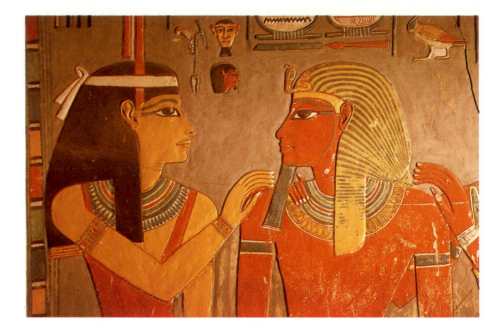

**The tomb of Horemheb in the Valley of the Kings presents admirable scenes of the pharaoh entertaining different goddesses.**

Following the religious reforms initiated by the mystical sovereign Akhenaten, the throne passed to Tutankhamun and then to the latter's vizier Ay. After these two short reigns, a general named Horemheb took the title of pharaoh (1343 BC). He returned Egypt to its former glory during the last twenty-seven years of the Eighteenth Dynasty. A novel form of wall painting—a polychrome sunk relief—was introduced in his tomb.

Above:
The pharaoh is being led to the afterlife by a graceful god.

Opposite:
This graceful portrait of the lovely goddess Hathor wearing the sun disk framed by cow horns displays an exceptionally high quality of workmanship.

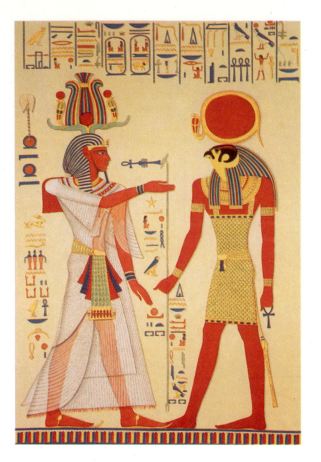

We find these aspects of a thirty-five-centuries-old civilization even more moving than the grandeur of the temples to the gods and the riches of the pharaonic funerary monuments. Nothing speaks better of a people than the inspired decorations in the tombs of nobles which sum up the fundamental convictions of generations of individuals–nobles and commoners alike. Death was an occasion for the Egyptians to exalt the graces of life. Many scenes display young and poignant couples in festive attire, united for eternity under the protection of the divine sun and assured of an afterlife filled with happiness and justice.

**Rosellini's 1820 survey of the tombs in the Valley of the Kings shows that the wall-paintings were surprisingly more colorful, than they are today.**

Above:
The pharaoh Merenptah paying homage to Re-Horakhte, the falcon sun-god. Thirteenth son and successor of Ramesses II (1235 BC), Merenptah was honored with a vast rock tomb at the end of the valley.

Opposite:
One of the superb scenes from King Sethos I's tomb. Here, the pharaoh is being led to Osiris, the god of the Dead, by Horus. Osiris, the symbol of resurrection, is seated on a throne. These scenes copied by the 19th-century Egyptologists Rosellini, Belzoni, and Champollion, have since lost most of their color.

118

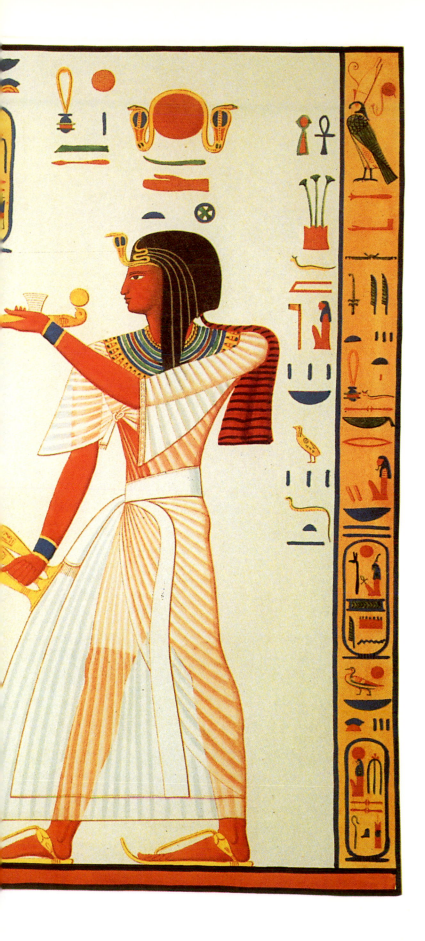

**A scene from the magnificent tomb of Ramesses III, copied by Rosellini.**

The pharaoh, performing rites, offers incense and libations to Osiris, Lord of the Dead and God of Resurrection, in the presence of Nut, the winged Goddess of the Heavens. Osiris's green color signifies that the deceased will grow again in the other world like vegetation after the flood.

# Duel between Amun and the Aten, between Thebes and Amarna

*During the ritual of the solar disc, Akhenaten and his wife*
*Nofreteti receive blessings from the small hands at the end*
*of the rays of the sun god.*
*(Egyptian Museum, Cairo)*

The two major developments marking the beginning of the New Kingdom were the territorial incursions by Theban troops with their war chariots into the heart of the Near East, establishing control over a vast empire in Asia, and the clergy's irresistible ascension to power in the Great Temples of Amun in the Upper Valley of the Nile. Considered as protector of the victorious armies, Amun the Sun God, benefited from considerable royal donations. The sovereigns generously manifested their gratitude to their tutelary divinity for each military success, and Amun attained the position of the State god of Thebes during the period of the expulsion of the Hyksos rulers from the Delta. Thebes thus became the rival city of Heliopolis where another sun god was revered under the names of Atum, Re or Khepri. The

**The heretic pharaoh Amenophis IV later took the name of Akhenaten and founded his own city at Tell el-Amarna.**

Akhenaten modified religious beliefs, expressing a monotheistic and abstract concept of a heavenly being, both King and Father. He also initiated a novel style of art by having the human figure depicted with realistic details. In this detail of a portrait of Akhenaten (1370-1360 BC) from a sandstone colossus at Karnak, the features are finer, the eyes longer, the lips fleshier and cheeks more hollowed out. (Museum of Ancient Egyptian Art, Luxor)

121

**The thoughtful expression of King Akhenaten.**

This statuette in limestone attests to the theological obsessions of a king who was divinely inspired. In contrast to his pacifistic leanings, Akhenaten wears the blue war helmet. (Egyptian Museum, Cairo)

Opposite:
King Akhenaten, Queen Nofreteti and one of their daughters offering libations to the sun disc. Bouquets of lotus flowers are placed on the sacrificial tables. (Egyptian Museum, Cairo)

supremacy of Thebes, which was now the royal capital and site of the palace of the pharaohs, accentuated religious antagonism, due in no small part to the extreme wealth of the Amun temples. The priests had laid their hands on so much fertile land and so many villages, that their domains grew as vast as those of the king. The pharaoh, however, reserved the right to appoint the chief priest of the temple and continued to maintain a certain control over the clergy.

## Syncretism and monotheism

Competition for religious dominance between the different sun cults opposed Thebes and Heliopolis for many centuries. This conflict demanded a solution and prompted the clergy to reconcile the different religious beliefs and doctrinal traditions throughout Egypt into a syncretistic system. The god Amun was therefore merged with Re. This amalgamation, however, proved insufficient to calm religious dissent. A further reorganization of solar cosmology and the establishment of a new celestial hierarchy seemed indispensable. A subtle genealogy of the principal gods was elaborated, grouping them into triads or groups of nine *(enneads)*. Revised legends of Creation were disseminated among the population to satisfy their curiosity, and theologians stretched their imagination to create new rituals.

The small group defending royal supremacy, composed of King Amenophis III and his court, cultivated a novel doctrine in an attempt to suppress the other cults. They placed the Aten–the solar disc with streaming rays–at the head of the religious hierarchy, rather than Atum, the creator of Heliopolis, or Amun-Re, the Hidden God of Thebes. The king regarded the Aten as the creative force of the universe manifested by the sun and proscribed all figurative representations of the god. This important aspect, from which all other mutations would arise, was the first monotheistic and abstract concept of divinity.

Conscious of the spiritual upheaval that would result from such a change in beliefs, King Amenophis III discreetly limited the cult of the Aten to certain members of his retinue. Although he was entirely immersed in Atenian mysticism, he showed tolerance and did not condemn the other forms of religion to which the rest of the Egyptian population was attached.

## The religious crisis under Akhenaten

At the death of King Amenophis III, his son Amenophis IV, ascended the throne. He shared the devout precepts of his father, but his own mystic exaltation soon expressed itself in vast building campaigns in other Egyptian villages and later on at a site further north. He erected temples to the glory of his new god and considered himself its prophet. Atenism then ceased to be an elitist cult.

King Amenophis IV, who reigned from *c.* 1372 to 1354 BC, wanted his subjects to share the beliefs which he embraced and for which he was the fervent spokesman. For that reason, he opposed the priests of the Amun temple at Thebes, who feared that their supremacy might be challenged and their proceeds confiscated by the followers of a new divinity. A schism was eventually provoked, leading to fanaticism and exclusion. The heretical king took the name Akhenaten ("One who Pleases the Disc") and decided to leave Thebes and settle in Middle Egypt. There, he founded a new city which he named Akhetaten ("Horizon of the Aten") at a site called Tell el-Amarna which become the capital of Egypt for a short time.

## The heretic pharaoh's constructions

The shrines devoted to the cult of the sun disc constituted a unique interlude in the history of pharaonic architecture. They differed in proportion, function and design more than in their mode of construction. After Akhenaten's death, the city and temples were razed to the ground and his name and that of his god were destroyed wherever they could be found. Few vestiges remain of Akhenaten's creations outside the city of Tell el-Amarna. The demolition was essentially the work of Ramesses II who, in order to hide all traces of the hated buildings, poured cement over the ruins, thus preserving them from total disappearance.

It is thanks to this dramatic destiny that we have been able to retrace the exact plans of Akhetaten's temples. His architects invented an original building technique. According to the Egyptologist Paul Barguet, after digging trenches outlining the shapes of the buildings to be erected, they then coated the trenches with a layer of white plaster; by stretching a soot-coated cord along the sides of the trenches and snapping it like a bowstring, they were able to mark the plan of the building's walls.

**A superb profile in relief on the tomb of general Imeneminet from the Amarnian Period.**

The flattened relief appears to have been carved by the same hand as the figures from the famed tomb of Rahmose at Sheikh abd el-Qurna. The high artistic quality of this profile in very fine sandstone is characteristic of the style at the end of the Eighteenth Dynasty. (Musée du Louvre, Paris)

Opposite:

**Cartouche of King Akhenaten sculpted in limestone.**
(Museo Egizio, Turin)

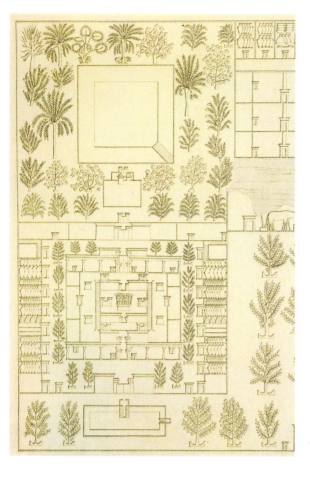

**Architecture of the Akhenaten period as represented in a tomb wall-painting from Tell el-Amarna.**

A garden with basins on each side of the sacred enclosure where different varieties of trees were cultivated. In the center, a courtyard bordered by storerooms of vases filled with food and beverages for offerings.

Opposite:
Crowned by the sun disc, a bird's-eye perspective shows the great temple of the Aten and its pylons. The broken lintels throughout the open edifice were designed so as not to cast shadows on the thoroughfare into the sanctuary. The altars and libation tables have been prepared for the worship of a single god. Many priests preside in the courtyards and under the porticos. These two reproductions, drawn one hundred and fifty years ago by Lepsius in the Tell el-Amarna necropolis, reveal the kind of buildings that were torn down during King Ramesses II's reign.

During recent excavations, traces of these lines were discovered under the layer of sand on which the stone foundations had been placed. It has been possible to reconstitute the elevation of these building by a careful study of the wall paintings and reliefs found in the Amarnian tombs.

## The solar temples of Akhetaten

A shrine for the adoration of the sun disc would not have been constructed like a sanctuary dedicated to a god represented by a statue or painted image and sheltered in the dark and mysterious depths of an inner sanctum. Although the solar rituals devoted to the Aten required similar sites and constructions to serve as houses of worship for communion with the sun, they no longer took place inside a room, but out of doors—a practice which was to bring about as profound a revolution in architecture as in theology.

Temples dedicated to the sun had existed since the Old Kingdom like those built by the priests of Heliopolis, and a tradition of solar altars, of which there is an example in the temple of Hatshepsut at Deir el-Bahri, was maintained until a late period. But these open-air sanctuaries inside temple precincts had not been created within a context of monotheism.

The great Aten sanctuary at Tell el-Amarna formed a vast complex that remains unique in the history of pharaonic architecture, and it is not surprising that its ground plan differs profoundly from that of the Karnak temple of Amun in Thebes. If the findings of archeologist are correct, the major house of worship of the solar disc, an immense roofless complex, measured 820ft (250m) long but only 130ft (40m) wide, and was oriented from west to east in order to follow the course of the sun.

In front of the massive pylon gateway marking the entrance, banners flew from six high masts. Through the gateway, the long prospect began with lateral porticos on both sides composed of two double columns pillars, followed by a succession of six broken-lintel doorways. Between each doorway, series of narrow open courtyards turned towards the central corridor leading to the open shrine held dozens of offering-tables disposed in orderly groups of four rows to the left and the right. Hundreds of cube-shaped brick altars, lining an enclosure measuring 2500 by 850 feet (760m x 270m), were put at the disposal of the faithful who came to make their modest

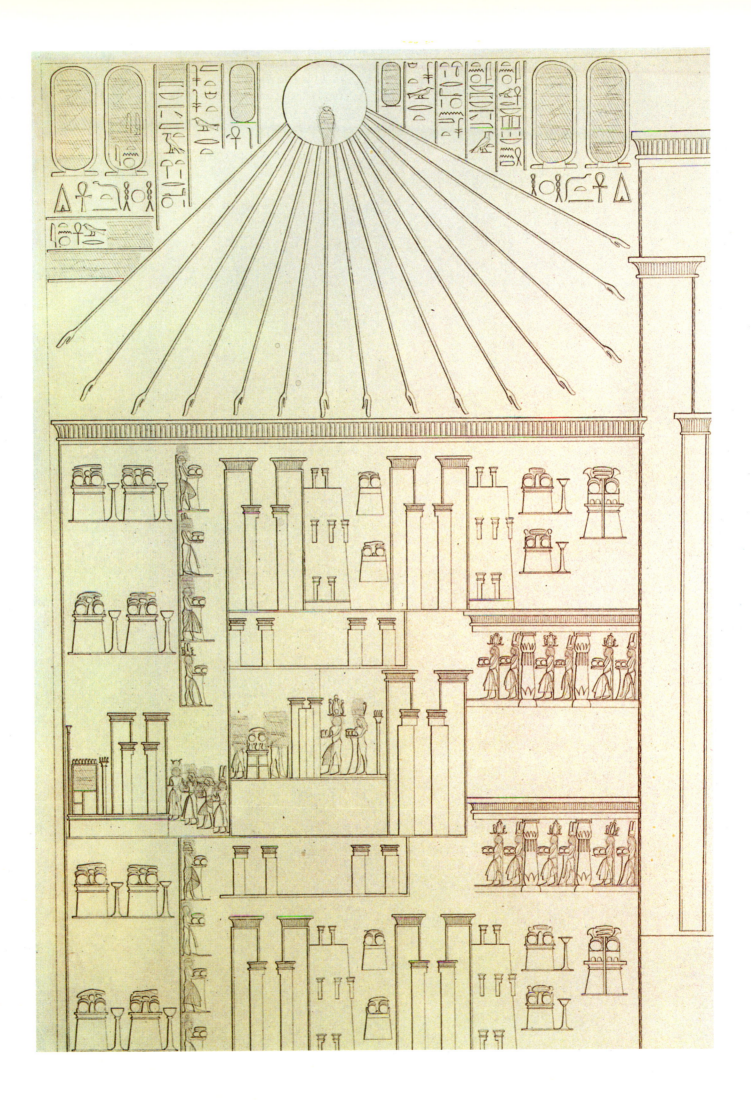

**The haughty profile of Queen Nofreteti.**

In typical Amarnian expressionistic style, the features of Queen Nofreteti have been subjected to certain physical distortions–a neck too thin for the head which is wearing an oversized headdress, exaggerated thick lips and strongly slanting eyes. The cobras normally placed on the forehead of the sovereign are fixed to the heavy mortar-shaped headdress and represent the Royal Uraeus. This work is from the Great Temple of the Aten at Tell el-Amarna. (Egyptian Museum, Cairo)

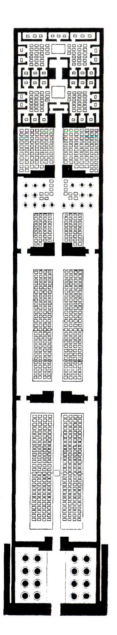

Floor plan of the Great Temple at Tell el-Amarna.

offerings. The furnishings attest to the importance which the sovereign gave to popular participation in the Atenian religion.

The king accompanied by his wife, the beautiful Queen Nofreteti, and their daughters conscientiously practiced their cult to the life-giving solar divinity, as we can see from the scenes sculpted in the sunk reliefs.

## The originality of Amarnian art

Except for the great temple, the architectural creations of the reign of Akhenaten are smaller; the blocks of sandstone (at Karnak) or limestone (at Tell el-Amarna) called *talatats*–an Arabic expression used by the workmen on digs–resembled bricks and measured only 20 x 10 x 8in (52 x 26 x 21,5cm). After the destruction of one of the Atenian sanctuaries, this material was re-used as fill for the construction of other walls and pylons. Many of the blocks presented a decorated face with painted scenes or reliefs. These fragments have allowed archeologists to reconstitute certain themes of Amarnian art (1367-1350 BC).

Digs on the Akhetaten site have uncovered frescos that adorned palaces and private houses, and nearby tombs present vestiges of decorations. Thanks to these remains, we know that this style was characterized by a great spontaneity, freedom and lucidity that broke with the conventional, often hieratic forms of traditional Egyptian art.

In this highly distinctive style, the king was depicted with a most peculiar physical appearance which, some have suggested, might be indicative of illness. He was represented with a thin face, squinting elongated eyes and an ecstatic smile; his body was deformed with a hollow chest, bulging belly, wide hips and round thighs like a woman. Queen Nofreteti was sculpted with a superb sensual femininity by their chief sculptor, Tuthmose. The royal princesses were portrayed with the same narrow face as their father, dainty features except for the sensual thick-lipped mouths, but the back of their skulls was deformed by unusual protuberances, resembling the statuary practices of certain primitive tribes. The scenes of the royal family allow us to intrude on an intimate family life represented with no concession to the ravages of time or physical peculiarities. The seemingly exaggerated style does not rule out a certain realism, not unlike that of the Minoan frescos of Thera (c. 1450 BC). The Amarnian style

Opposite:

**An unfinished portrait in quartzite of beautiful Queen Nofreteti.**

This work was somehow spared the idiosyncrasies of Amarnian art. The absolute perfection of the proud face and the profound spirituality of the expression caught by the sculptor Tuthmose is very moving. The head whose crown has only been sketched, would have received a voluminous headdress made out of another material. The slight coloration, with the highlighted eyes outlined in ink gives the Queen an elusive appearance.
(Egyptian Museum, Cairo)

**King Akhenaten and Queen Nofreteti had five daughters.**

Their daughters were often associated with scenes of family life and worship. This sculpted portrait of a child with thick lips in a typical Amarnian style was discovered in the house of a chief sculptor Tuthmose at Tell el-Amarna.
This exaggerated form of the skull continued into the Tutankhamun period, as confirmed by the following illustration.
(Egyptian Museum, Cairo)

131

**King Tutankhamun as a child, when he was still called Tutankhaten.**

The young king displays the same skull deformation as King Akhenaten's daughters. This wooden polychrome head, found in the tomb discovered by Lord Carnarvon and Howard Carter in the Valley of the Kings in 1922, shows a boy seemingly concerned by the pressures of life in a troubled age. (Egyptian Museum, Cairo)

Opposite:

**King Tutankhamun**

When he came of age, Tutankhamun re-established the cult of Amun and abandoned the Amarnian style. He preferred the traditional idealized and radiant features. The only indication of the former style on this colossal alabaster statue from Karnak (where the King sits to the right of the god Amun) is the eyes, which are almost as narrow as those of Akhenaten. Nonetheless the Amarnian period seems to be a thing of the past. (Museo Egizio, Turin)

is unmistakable, yet it poses questions which have yet to be satisfactorily answered.

## The restoration of the cult of Amun

King Akhenaten's exile and his preoccupation with religious questions led to a decline of pharaonic authority, paving the way to internal disorder which was exacerbated by the weakened central administration and failing agricultural production.

The reign of the heretical king disintegrated into chaos and was succeeded by that of a prince named Tutankhaten, who resided first in Tell el-Amarna but soon manifested a desire to return to the traditional religious forms. After three years of hesitation he rejected the cult of the Aten entirely, adopted the name of King Tutankhamun and began the work of restoring the former rituals. Paradoxically this minor young pharaoh, who died before reaching the age of twenty in 1345 BC, came to have the greatest posthumous glory–thanks to the treasures found in 1922 by Carnarvon and Carter in an otherwise modest tomb in the Valley of the Kings. The masterpieces found in abundance around the gold sarcophagus and in the chambers crammed with objects often attest to the survival of Amarnian forms.

At the end of the religious crisis, General Horemheb, backed by the Theban clergy, acceded to the throne in 1333 BC and condemned the memory of Akhenaten, had his name struck from the royal tables and prepared the advent of the glorious Nineteenth Dynasty of the Ramessides.

**The treasure of King Tutankhamun.
An extraordinary discovery of the riches of
a minor sovereign.**

The opulence of the funerary belongings of this
transitory ruler who died at the age of twenty
stirs the imagination. What then were the
possessions of kings who reigned for decades?

Above:
The small wooden tabernacle covered with
sheets of decorated or embossed gold is an
admirable cult object. In spite of its small size
(20in, 50cm), it includes some of the
characteristic Egyptian architectural
features—cavetto cornice and cambered roof.
(Egyptian Museum, Cairo)

Left:
A solid gold miniature replica of King
Tutankhamun's sarcophagus was part of a
group of four identical coffins that held the
King's entrails in the canopic shrine.
This life-size illustration shows the superb
cloisonné work of the Egyptian goldsmiths
around 1340 BC. (Egyptian Museum, Cairo)

King Tutankhamun owed his impressive treasures to the craftsmanship and enthusiasm of his goldsmiths.

This magnificent cloisonné pectoral reproducing the façade of a sanctuary displays the two goddesses Nephthys and Isis spreading their protective wings over a Djed Pillar, symbol of stability and permanence. This jewel had the function of a talisman. (Egyptian Museum, Cairo)

Opposite:

**Watchdog of the Necropolis, the god Anubis guards the entrance of the canopic chamber of Tutankhamun's tomb.**

This three-foot-long (1m) wooden sculpture represents a wild desert dog and not a jackal. The animal, with elongated ears, pointed muzzle and small feet, roams at night and represents the master of the City of the Dead. The statue is covered with black varnish highlighted with gold; the eyes are in alabaster and obsidian. (Egyptian Museum, Cairo)

Following pages:

**Two magnificent reproductions by Richard Lepsius of a wall-painting found in a tomb from the period of the reign of Tutankhamun.**

These beautiful frescos were copied inside the tomb of Amenemope near Sheikh abd el-Qurna in the middle of the 19th century.
Page 138. The deceased is shown fanning King Tutankhamun. The King, seated on his throne in a columned *naos* surmounted by a cobra frieze, wears the blue war helmet and holds the flail and scepter as well as the *ankh*.
Page 139. The majestic pharaoh sits in his aedicule in front of a table laden with offerings from which hang two panther skins. The tray above holds exotic gold objects displaying Nubians, giraffes, palm trees, tributes in the form of gold rings and vases containing balsamic oils.

# THE GLORY OF THE RAMESSIDES

## A FRENZY OF CONSTRUCTION

*A superb relief of Sethos I at Abydos. The king officiates
in his temple wearing a simple skullcap adorned
with the Royal Uraeus.*

The privilege of founding the Nineteenth Dynasty (1306-1186 BC) was bestowed upon Ramesses I, a general who was already an old man when he acceded to the throne for a short period of two years. Nonetheless, his name was given to one of the most glorious eras of the New Kingdom: the Ramesside Period.

This great warrior distinguished himself by re-establishing order in a territory in central Anatolia (part of present-day Turkey) under Hittite rule, as well as many other regions where Egyptian authority had been allowed to decline during the Amarnian Age. Discovering that the heretical king Amenophis IV (Akhenaten) was so engrossed in his religious reforms that he neglected his Asian territories, the Hittites launched a campaign into Northern

Opposite:

**The second hypostyle hall of the temple of King Sethos I at Abydos.**

Photographed in a soft light, this vestibule, built around 1320 BC, is formed by thirty-six smooth papyrus-bud columns, crowned by simple abaci, except for the third row on the right standing on slightly higher bases. From this period on, the hypostyle hall became regular feature in Egyptian temple architecture.

Syria and annexed Mitani, a mountainous region of the upper Tigris and Euphrates. Carchemish, a strategic stronghold, fell after a show of resistance. As a result, the expanding Hittite nation became a menace to the Egyptian possessions in the Near East.

It was Sethos I, son of King Ramesses I, who brought grandeur back to the pharaonic institution. He had been invited by his father to take part in government at an early age and became the true founder of the dynasty. Starting in 1312 BC, this pharaoh embarked on a series of campaigns and was able to recover the fortress of Kadesh, a key position in the defense of the Egyptian vassal states in Palestine and Syria. He then signed a pact of non-aggression with the Hittite king, Mursilis II. Besides his military accomplishments, King Sethos I revivified Egyptian art and engaged in many building projects pursued after his death by his own son the great Ramesses II (1290-1224 BC).

The pact that Egypt had drawn up with the Hittites did not survive King Sethos I's death. Five years after ascending to the throne, King Ramesses II, anxious to recover his lost Syrian possessions, resumed hostilities in the Near East. He had been misled by informants who told him that the Hittite king, Muwatallis, was busy fighting against northern invaders in Anatolia. Leading the Egyptian armies, he advanced upon the city of Kadesh that stood on a hill between two branches of the Orontes River in Northern Syria. The Hittites attacked by surprise at dawn, provoking a memorable battle. From this point on the texts differ, for there are two versions of the outcome; according to the Hittites, Muwatallis won, but the Egyptians also claimed victory. The Pentaour Poems and many reliefs carved on the walls of Egyptian temples celebrate this battle with symbolic representations of the pharaoh in his chariot single-handedly charging the Hittites troops. The truth probably combines elements from both sides. King Ramesses II with a few gallant warriors was able to escape from the ambush, thus denying Muwatallis absolute victory.

The two kingdoms signed a truce, but later on, a revolt fomented by vassal states set off another military campaign in the area. The Hittites were eventually defeated (c. 1288 BC) and another treaty was drawn up to establish a balance of power between the two belligerents. Peace was finally sealed by the successive marriages of King Ramesses II to several Hittite princesses.

Towards the end of a reign that seemed to have dragged on for too long, the great pharaoh lost his grip over the

142

**Sanctuary dedicated to the mysteries of Osiris, Master of the Other World.**

In the center of the Abydos temple, Sethos I built a group of transversal rooms forming a small hypostyle sanctuary devoted to Osiris, the God of Resurrection. The atmosphere is one of contemplation. The wall paintings illustrate the procedures of the daily offerings. The cylindrical columns are merely topped with simple abaci.

**Detail from a scene in an Abydos temple chapel.**

The colors have kept a definite freshness, for the rooms were entirely engulfed in the sands for a long period of time. The scene shows the king holding the royal insignia and worshipping Horus, seated on a throne.

political situation and found himself confronted with hostile pressures from opposing factions. Foreign rulers cast envious looks on the rich cities of the Nile Valley while overlords stirred up the populations and antagonistic tendencies endangered the unity of the nation. The king's authority dwindled and, unable to enforce treaties, he lost control over the annexed territories. In spite of all this, Egypt was still perceived by its neighbors as an invincible empire yet in many ways it had become a besieged fortress.

### An age of great works

As Ramesses II felt the need for a military base in Lower Egypt, he founded the fortified city of Per-Ramesses in the vicinity of Avaris that had once been the capital of the Hyksos. Closer to the theater of operations he could counter Hittite expansionism and put a stop to raids from the Peoples of the Sea. Defending the strategic position of the passage from Palestine into the Delta, Per-Ramesses became the main residence of several kings of the Nineteenth Dynasty and was said to have been a magnificent city. Egypt was also under threat on its western flank. Ramesses II therefore established a series of garrisons on the western border of the Delta to control incursions from the turbulent Libyan nomads

Many new cities were founded along the Nile Valley, bringing about a complete social renewal. Some of them, were set up as administrative or military centers, and laid out on a right-angled network, a tradition in Egyptian city planning that went back to the Middle Kingdom (Illahun) and even to the Old Kingdom. Orthogonal plans also remind us of necropolises that were conceived as idealized reproductions of a pharaonic city, such as King Djoser's funerary complex at Saqqara and the geometrical grouping of mastabas around the pyramids.

During the Ramesside Dynasties, the kings were able to carry out phenomenal building programs. The period starting with King Sethos I's accession to the throne and ending at Ramesses II's death is probably the richest in architectural creations. Monuments built during these years are both colossal and magnificent, and their construction transformed the Nile Valley into an immense building site. Sethos I built, among others, the impressive Temple at Sheikh abd el-Qurna, the lavish memorial Temple of Abydos, and the formidable hypostyle hall of the Great Temple of Amun at Karnak (started during the Eighteenth Dynasty). Ramesses II built the Ramesseum

**Sethos I offering libations contained in a gold ewer with a pouring lip.**

Detail from a delicate raised relief decorating the Hall of Ancestors, which displays cartouches of the seventy-six previous rulers, demonstrating the extraordinary artistic ability at the time of the first Ramesside Kings. The vulture symbolizing the protective goddess Nekhbet flies above the king's head.

and two rock-hewn temples with majestic statues at Abu Simbel along the Nile in Nubia as well as many obelisks and sanctuaries in Upper and Middle Egypt.

In all the principal sites, inscriptions, reliefs, wall paintings, and hieratic statuary from this period can be found although they were sometimes usurped from earlier monuments. These tangible remains help us to grasp the scope of the undertakings of the Nineteenth Dynasty master-builders. Most of these works were carved with Ramesses II's cartouche and displayed his complete name: Usermaatre Setempre Meramun, "The One God Re brings to life."

### The Temple of King Sethos I at Abydos

The curious cenotaphs built by kings of the Old Kingdom in the southern city of Abydos can be considered as the counterparts of the royal sepulchers in the northern sites of Giza, Saqqara and Dahshur. These funerary monuments provided the pharaohs with the means to assert their authority over the Two Lands.

It was thus in the ancient city of Abydos in Upper Egypt that Sethos I (*c.* 1300 BC) chose to build one of the most significant monuments of ancient Egypt, an impressive complex designed as both a mansion for the gods and a house for immortality. It was not, strictly speaking, a mortuary temple but a sanctuary planned according to a totally new concept. He had already erected his own mortuary temple at Sheikh abd el-Qurna not far from his great tomb hewn in the cliffs of the Valley of Kings. His Abydos complex therefore served two sacred functions: it was devoted to the seven deities with whom Sethos I wished to be associated (Amun-Re, Horus, Re-Horakhte or Harmachis, Ptah, Isis, Osiris, and the king himself); and, it commemorated the death and resurrection of Osiris. The ground-plan of the sanctuary reflects this dual purpose, for the Osireion was a smaller separate temple behind the great temple.

The gateway pylons and peristyle courtyard of the main temple have been destroyed, but the two hypostyle halls and inner chapels are in a remarkable state of conservation. Many traces of the original paint have remained in a miraculous state of freshness. The first hypostyle hall with twelve rows of double papyrus bud columns (25ft; 7.5m high) forming seven aisles led to a second hypostyle hall where the same arrangement was repeated, except that the twelve rows were now three

**Behind and below the temple of Abydos lie the remains of a monument called the Osireion, now partly under water.**

The enormous pink granite pillars of the edifice devoted to the worship of Osiris evoke the structures of the valley temple of King Khephren at Giza. It was constructed as a subterranean cenotaph–a place of re-birth devoted to the God of the Deceased.

148

**Scene decorating the subterranean corridor that leads down to the Osireion at Abydos.**

A procession of figures hauls the divine barque transporting the naos-cabin which contains a representation of Khnum, the ram-headed god described in a text from the *Book of the Gates*. These scenes, sculpted in sandstone, were executed during the reign of King Merenptah, heir and successor of Ramesses II.

Opposite:

**A kneeling offering-bearer in the temple of King Ramesses II at Abydos.**

This superb relief from the semi-eroded sanctuary has preserved vibrant colors. The red dress, the gold vases, and the hair of lapis lazuli form a particularly harmonious composition. This detail allows us to imagine what pharaonic architecture must have looked like highlighted with vivid colors.

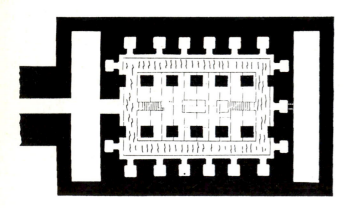

Plan of Sethos I's Osireion at Abydos.

columns deep and the seven aisles of this second hall served as vestibules for the seven inner chapels. A processional barque housing the statue of the deity stood on a pedestal in the center of each chapel (16 x 32ft; 5 x 10m). The statue of the god was shown to the worshipers during the feast-day celebration. All the doors of the chapels were false with the exception of one beyond which lay a small hypostyle hall with twelve columns adjacent to a four-columned square room leading to the Osireion.

The atmosphere of awe and mystery, best achieved with a minimum of light, can still be felt in these halls for their stone roof-slabs have remained in place. The light falling at an angle caresses the lovely reliefs, enhancing the delicate polychromy and highlighting their exquisite drawing. Such a high degree of refinement, blending Amarnian influences with traditional forms, could only be attained through a perfect mastery of style. Very few pharaonic sanctuaries can compete with the temple of Sethos II in conveying the magic qualities of a sacred building.

A wing attached to the southeast end (the temple was built on an unusual L-shaped ground-plan), housed the treasures, the sacrificial slaughterhouse, and the Hall of Ancestors, which displayed the famous list of Kings carved in relief on the limestone wall. Sethos I himself is portrayed burning incense in front of the cartouches of Egypt's seventy-six previous rulers stretching from the time of King Menes—the mythical founder of the First dynasty—to his own day.

### The Osireion: a cosmological sanctuary

The Osireion, which is said to have been visited by the Greek geographer Strabo (c 90 BC), and by Hadrian, the Roman emperor (AD 117-138) lay below ground level in an open area behind the temple. It was approached by a long sloping subterranean corridor whose limestone walls were decorated with mythological scenes taken from the *Book of the Gates* and the *Book of the Caverns*. These beautiful reliefs date from the reign of King Merenptah. Transverse vestibules with saddleback roofs flanked the north and south sides of the actual shrine. One of the vestibules was decorated with reliefs illustrating astronomical concepts such as celestial bodies under a representation of the sky goddess Nut; on another wall, a text described the construction of a solar dial.

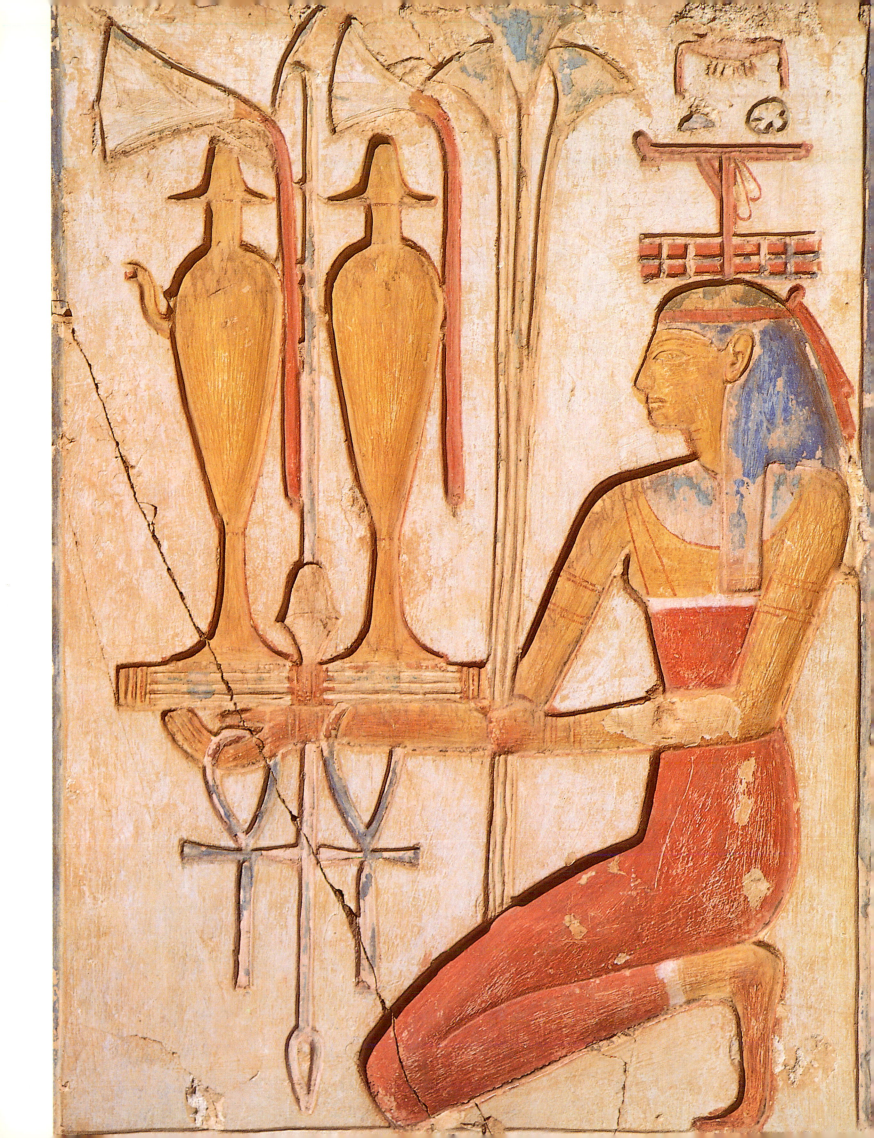

The shrine itself sat on a rectangular islet (72 x 40ft; 22 x 12m) surrounded by a moat fed by ground water and lay at the center of a vast rectangular hall (164 x 105ft; 50 x 32m) bordered by seventeen chapels. Massive pink granite blocks and monolithic pillars constituted this impressive structure reminiscent of the trabeated porticos of the valley temple of King Khephren at Giza which was built some 1500 years earlier.

Curiously enough, no bridge spanned the moat and it is not clear how the islet was reached. Steps descending into the water could have been used to cross over, or a gangway lowered on special occasions. Whether the water-bound building was partly or wholly roofed is unknown; perhaps the islet had to remain in direct contact with the open skies for ritualistic purposes.

In the Osireion the symbols of creation, life, death, and resurrection were intimately associated with the solar cycle and with the circumpolar stars regarded as the "Imperishable Ones." A design of this type might have fulfilled a magical function enabling the priests to establish a strong cosmic relationship between the Primeval Waters, symbolized by the moat, and the Primeval Mound, or the seat of Creation, symbolized by the islet which represented both Osiris' tomb and birth place. As the master of stars and of the zodiac, the pharaoh linked his fate to the deceased and the resurrected god Osiris and was entrusted with sacred astronomy as part of his attributes.

## One of the Wonders of the World

The great hypostyle hall of the temple of Amun at Karnak was often listed in ancient times as one of the Seven Wonders of the World. Begun during the Eighteenth Dynasty and completed under the Ramessides, this marvelous and gigantic structure (334 x 174ft; 102m x 53m) enclosed the area between the second and third pylon of the temple, once an open courtyard. The hall was reached through the second pylon (built under Horemheb) and was entirely roofed with stone slabs supported by 134 columns. Light was admitted through clerestory windows located 75ft (23m) above a central nave bordered by twelve bell-shaped columns, each weighing some 500 tons. These columns probably date back to the reign of Amenophis III and are reminiscent of the double colonnade built by this same king in the Temple of Luxor. The remaining sixty-one papyrus-bud columns 49ft

**Ramesses II in all his glory.**

Superb basanite statue of the ruling king, wearing the War Crown (*khepresh*). Champollion enthusiastically called this work "The Apollo Belvedere of Egyptian art." (Museo Egizio, Turin)

Opposite above:
The central alley of the great hypostyle hall with its columns surmounted by bell-shaped capitals was created by Amenophis III at the Amun temple in Karnak. Ramesses II had his own cartouches superimposed over those of former kings when he completed the decoration of the lateral hypostyle halls housing the sacred barque.

Opposite below:
View of the Amun temple at Karnak from the east bank of the sacred lake. In the background, the first pylon; in front, spreads the great hypostyle hall constructed by: Amenophis III, Horemheb, Sethos I, and Ramesses II.

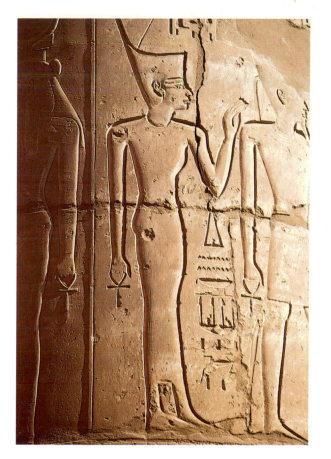

**The great temple of Amun at Karnak evokes a vast petrified forest with light playing among the massive columns.**

In the vast hall with its shafts tapering up from swollen bases and surmounted by closed papyrus-bud capitals, the 122-column edifice, begun by Horemheb but completed only at the beginning of the Nineteenth Dynasty, was decorated with sculpted scenes during the period of King Sethos I and Ramesses II. The latter literally covered the walls with his cartouches. The sunken reliefs sculpted on the heavy stone supports (which have unfortunately lost their roof slabs) depict a procession of gods.

**The temples of Abu Simbel were removed and reconstructed to escape submersion.**

*Above:*
The great temple as seen by Lepsius in 1845, still partially buried under sand.

*Below:*
A bird's-eye view of the rock-carved temples (since rebuilt).

*Opposite:*
Entirely sculpted out of the cliff facing the Nile at Abu Simbel, the colossal seated figures portray a triumphal Ramesses II wearing the Double Crown (*Pschent*).

(15m) high, begun under Horemheb and finished by the Ramessides, complete the structure on either side of the nave.

This famous hall was not planned to receive many faithful, for it served as a repository for the sacred barque. Its enormous proportions perfectly illustrate the megalomania that affected the Ramessides master-builders, who more than other Egyptian kings, destroyed the works of their predecessors, usurped royal monuments, and marked their names on temples to the gods built by others.

### The temples of Abu Simbel

Ramesses II set no bounds to his ambition in raising monuments to his own glory. He chose an isolated site in Nubia beyond the second cataract of the Nile as the location for the temple of Abu Simbel. The proportions of this monument are grandiose and extravagant. The conventional temple pylon was replaced here by a vast façade entirely cut out of the sandstone cliff and preceded by four seated figures of the king 69ft (21m) high also carved out of the rock. These royal effigies facing the rising sun blended perfectly into the surrounding landscape. Both figures sat enthroned like the two Colossi of Memnon that once stood in front of Amenophis III's temple at Western Thebes.

The ancient architects of Abu Simbel abandoned their traditional methods of construction with blocks and carved out their temple directly from the rock like sculptors carve a statue. The actual temple tunneled into the cliff to reach a depth of more than 180ft (55m). The inside space *(hypogeum)* was no less impressive than the façade and also demonstrated the extraordinary mastery of the Egyptian architects. Eight large Osiride pillars displayed the pharaoh's figure frozen in a sarcophagus-like attitude, wearing the Double Crown (*pschent*), ceremonial beard, scepter, and flail. Standing in a double row, these pillars adorned a vestibule that led into another pillared hall. At the back of the temple, four seated statues representing the deified Ramesses with Ptah, Amun-Re, and Re-Horakhte were also carved directly in the rock. On either side of the main hall, small side-chambers plunged in obscurity provided space to store the temple treasure, cult objects and ritual offerings.

The sandstone walls on each side of the vestibule were carved with raised reliefs extolling the military exploits of Ramesses II; in the company of almost 1500 figures of

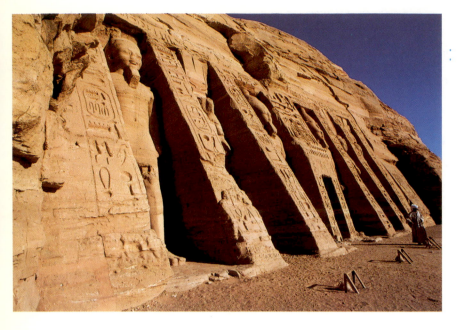

**The sculpted architecture of the temples of Abu Simbel were executed in homage to Queen Nofretari and Ramesses II.**

Above:
The rock-carved Small Temple was dedicated to the chief consort of the pharaoh. The six façade figures standing on either side of the entrance include four colossal statues of the King and two of the Queen, represented exceptionally in the same scale as her husband.

Opposite:
The Great Temple, also hewn out of the rock, exhibits four colossal figures of King Ramesses II seated on his throne, one of which crumbled in antiquity. The figures, turned toward the rising sun, today face an interior sea–Lake Nasser–which spreads over several hundred miles in Upper Egypt and Sudan. Both of these immense sanctuaries of self-glorification were built between 1300 and 1250 BC.

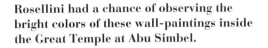
**Rosellini had a chance of observing the bright colors of these wall-paintings inside the Great Temple at Abu Simbel.**

Today the colors have faded. The reliefs depict Ramesses II commemorating his victories, especially the one against the Hittites at Kadesh on the Orontes River. Represented successively are: (above) a bold war chariot leaving for the campaign; (below) the massacre of the Asians; (center and opposite) the pharaoh, still armed, offering his African prisoners to the gods. On the left, the great god Amun of Karnak; on the right, his "associate," the goddess Mut; in the center, the deified king who wears on his head the horn insignia of Amun form a triad. This same headdress was used a thousand years later by Alexander the Great when he returned in triumph from the Oasis of Siuah.

**The Osiride pillars bordering the *pronaos* in the Great Temple of Abu Simbel.**

Carved in the rock, these colossal emblematic sculptures represent Ramesses II with his royal insignia. They stand about 33 ft (10 m) high.

soldiers, the king is shown spearing foes, smiting an enemy chieftain mounted on a chariot, charging a fortress, and inspecting piles of severed hands; certain episodes from the mighty battle of Kadesh were also described in detail. The colors of what remains of these reliefs are still visible but have probably lost much of the vividness they still had when Rosellini and Champollion copied them at the beginning of last century.

At a small distance to the north of his temple, Ramesses II ordered another smaller rock-carved temple to be built in honor of his royal consort, Queen Nofretari, and dedicated to the goddess Hathor. The façade was fronted by four colossal standing statues of the deified king and two figures of the queen, represented on the same scale as her husband. Inside, a vestibule contained six Hathoric columns and led to a sanctuary with a niche housing a statue representing the Queen—in the bovine form of the goddess Hathor—with tiny figures of her children by her feet.

The high Aswan Dam which eventually opened in 1971 would have completely obliterated these vestiges of the Ramesside grandeur. The temples of Abu Simbel were moved to another location and replaced in their exact position; their exemplary rescue was an admirable, an almost unimaginable achievement.

**Inside the Nofretari *speos* at Abu Simbel.**

The face of the pillars bordering the central alley are decorated with
representations of Hathor. The three other faces depict tutelary divinities.
This room forms a vestibule (*pronaos*) measuring 36 square ft (11 m²)
and is entirely carved out of the cliff. In the sanctuary devoted to Hathor,
the King and Queen are shown presiding over sacrifices. On both sides of
the far entrance wall, Ramesses II is depicted crushing his prisoners'
skulls.

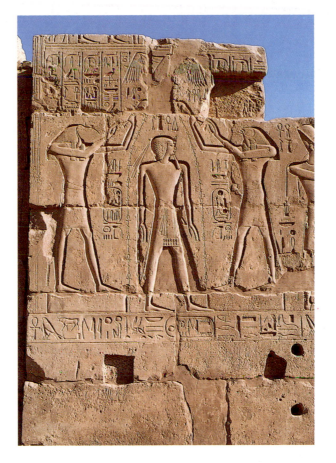

**Reliefs and obelisks bear
cartouches honoring
Ramesses II.**

This scene shows the young
king receiving a divine
"baptism" in the form of the
"keys of life" pouring out from
ewers held by the gods Thoth
and Horus.

Opposite:
The stone needle of the obelisk
of Ramesses II at the Amun-Re
temple in Luxor was topped
by a pyramidion covered with
gold or electrum, a symbol of
sunlight. This obelisk is the
twin of the one offered by
Mehemet Ali to King Louis-
Philippe: it has graced the
Place de la Concorde in Paris
since in 1836.

# FUNERARY TEMPLES OF THEBES

## AND RAMESSIDE PALACES

*The Ramesseum, a thousand-year-old palace in Western Thebes, the mortuary temple of an immortal pharaoh.*

The tradition of separating the tomb site from the funerary temple, instituted by the Tuthmosis and Amenophis kings at the beginning of the New Kingdom, was widely observed during the Nineteenth Dynasty, as we have seen. The most interesting feature of these temples is the fact that they were planned and erected during a single reign. Even if they did not reach completion before the death of the ruler, they were seldom modified or added to by his successors. In keeping with cult requirements, very few architectural changes were permitted; this has permitted us to follow the evolution of these religious edifices and to study the types of options and interior arrangements chosen. For this reason, the Ramesside monuments of Thebes are

Opposite:

**King Ramesses II making sacrifices to the god Amun, who wears a plumed head-dress, in the Ramesseum's first hypostyle hall.**

Sandstone reliefs in the funerary temple of the King boast of Egyptian war victories with scenes of marching troops, assaults on fortresses, and chariot battles. Shown here on a pillar is a cartouche of Ramesses II crowned by the sun and flanked by royal cobras.

**The mass of the hypostyle hall of the Ramesseum at the foot of the Theban Hills.**

As the surrounding wall has disappeared. columns are visible behind the Osiride colonnade. On the left, the initial section of the west portico belonging to a second courtyard.

Opposite:
Facing the hypostyle hall, a row of four other Osiride columns in front of a wall decorated with reliefs depicting the Battle of Kadesh. On the extreme right, the ruins of the great colossus of Ramesses II, a granite monolith that originally must have weighed some 1200 tons.

particularly informative, for they display the standard temple design that was still in use in the 3rd century when the ancient Egyptian civilization came to an end.

## The temple of Sethos I at Sheikh abd el-Qurna

Across the Nile from Thebes, Sethos I erected a temple devoted to his own cult and to that of his father Ramesses I. This sanctuary, like the one in Abydos, has lost its two vestibules and pylons, but a small six-columned hypostyle hall surrounded by chapels remains intact.

To the right lies a courtyard containing the solar altar, to the left, the ritual chambers dedicated to Ramesses I, and at the end, the ruins of several more rooms. The ensemble, supported by ungainly, thick columns has rather heavy proportions, which are a far cry from the elegance of the Abydos temple and the decoration is as disappointing as the architecture.

To the south of the temple, a sacred lake surrounded a flagstoned islet representing the primeval hill similar to the Osireion of Abydos–apparently a recurrent theme.

## The Ramesseum of Thebes

Standing inside a vast brick enclosure, the Temple of Ramesses II, 277ft (300m) long and 167ft (200m) wide, was built by an architect named Penre according to a conventional temple plan with two pylons, two peristyle courtyards, a hypostyle hall, a series of vestibules and secondary rooms, a barque shrine, and a sanctuary. Behind the temple are numerous well-preserved vaulted mudbrick storerooms.

Although in an advanced state of ruin today, the Ramesseum offers an superb view of the many heavily decorated halls that were formally intended to remain in obscurity. The portico leading into the hypostyle hall was approached by three ramps, originally preceded by a colossus measuring some 55ft (17m) tall and weighing 1100 tons. The pylons were carved with reliefs showing scenes from the Battle of Kadesh, a common temple theme. In the raised hypostyle hall more carved reliefs illustrated the capture of the Hittite fortress of Dapur in Northern Syria. Only 29 of the original 48 sandstone papyrus-bud columns forming the hall have survived. These, accompanied by rows of bell-shaped capitals, formed a broad central nave with a higher ceiling, similar

to the one at the Temple of Amun at Karnak. There are ruins of a second hypostyle hall supported by eight shafts which was aligned with two other halls of similar size of which no trace remains. The inner sanctum has also disappeared.

This enormous ruin, with its broken statues and gutted chambers spreading on the edge of a fertile plain is not devoid of charm. However, the Ramesseum's major attraction is the Tomb of Ozymandias (a corruption of Usermaatre, King Ramesses' coronation name) rendered famous by the ancient Greek historian Diodorus and much later by Shelley's "King of Kings."

Within the perimeter of the temple lay a small palace of Ramesses II, which was fitted with the "Window of Appearances," a balcony where the sovereign would appear before the faithful to distribute honors and receive tribute. As we will see, this architectural formula, probably handed down from royal practices established by Akhenaten at Tell el-Amarna, developed widely under Ramesses III at Medinet Habu.

### The mudbrick arches

The barrel vaults forming storerooms situated to the north of the Ramesseum and devoted to religious practices, were made of three or four layers of mudbrick voussoirs, a building technique that has surprisingly maintained its structural stability through the ages. These storerooms offer us an opportunity to study this type of building technique, and it is possible to make a comparison between the superposed layers of bricks and somewhat similar methods of making laminated materials today.

This very efficient barrel vaulting is absent from the stone edifices of pharaonic Egypt. Only the corbel vaults (false vaults), such as those in the seven chapels with arcuated roofs of the temple of Abydos, were fashioned in stone. True mudbrick arches appeared as early as the Sixth Dynasty at Giza in the halls of certain mastabas and would inspire civil architecture throughout the later periods. They were also used for the temple of Amenophis III and the sanctuary erected by his architect, Amenhotep-son-of-Hapu.

Why did the master-builders of the Nile Valley use mudbrick for the construction of arches rather than stone? Perhaps they were reluctant to face the complicated techniques needed to cut stone for such architectural feats, and in the absence of sufficiently

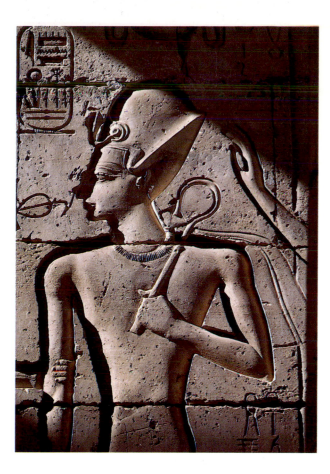

**Many sunk reliefs of the crowned sovereign adorned the Ramesseum.**

The mortuary temple was erected to commemorate the deified conqueror.

Opposite:
The arches of the storehouses to the north which are part of the temple and devoted to religious practices, are made of three or four layers of mudbrick voussoirs, a building technique that has maintained its structural stability surprisingly well through the ages. This very efficient barrel vaulting is absent from stone edifices in pharaonic architecture.

Following page:

**The great relief of the Battle of Kadesh.**

Egyptian and Hittite chariots engaged on a battlefield strewn with the bodies of the dead and wounded. This scene covers an entire wall of the Ramesseum.

sturdy wooden beams, they were forced to adapt themselves to this type of medium.

## The reign of Ramesses III

After a long reign, Ramesses II was succeeded by his thirteenth son, Merenptah, marking the beginning of the decline of the dynasty. The usual disorders again came to the fore, this time from the Libyan tribes menacing the western boundaries of Egypt. The Egyptians wanted not just to construct fortresses but wished to wipe out their enemy. They were finally able to subdue the semi-nomadic tribes, thus bringing the pharaoh some respite. But a reversal of alliances took place in Asia, and King Merenptah found it expedient to re-arm the Hittite troops and to permit them to fight against even more fearsome contenders, the Assyrians.

The long period of prosperity and flourishing trade came to an end in the last decades of the 13th century BC. The kings continued their vain attempts to maintain order in the face of invasions by the Peoples of the Sea, which brought widespread destruction on the eastern Mediterranean lands and to the realm of the pharaohs. A Palestinian ruler even ascended the Egyptian throne around 1205 BC.

Restoration came about during the Twentieth Dynasty thanks to Ramesses III who repelled the invaders on all fronts. He was not just a skillful tactician and clever politician, but also an enthusiastic builder who resumed great building projects and erected a vast royal shrine.

## Medinet Habu, the divine city of King Ramesses III

The monumental temple complex of Medinet Habu, in a remarkable state of conservation, is a perfect illustration of the principles of New Kingdom architecture. The design was based on a series of protective enclosures, one inside the next, until reaching the inner sanctum. This configuration of consecutive ramparts merging temple, palace and fortress guaranteed security and tranquillity to the shrine. Similarly, the deceased king was protected by a succession of sarcophagi in granite, limestone, gold, silver, and finally laid in a series of wooden coffins, finely adjusted to nestle one inside the other like Russian dolls. This disposition was also closely related to the structure of the world as described by Egyptian cosmology, with the Primeval Waters acting as a protective moat surrounding

**The Great Temple of Medinet Habu erected by Ramesses II in Thebes to commemorate his victories.**

The edifice lying beyond the sacred lake, preceding the large pylon appears intact from a distance. It was built around 1190 BC. On the left are the structures of a smaller temple raised at the time of Queen Hatshepsut and King Tuthmosis III.

Below:
The portico bordering the second courtyard of the temple of Ramesses III at Medinet Habu. The proportions are heavy and the reliefs somewhat cursory.

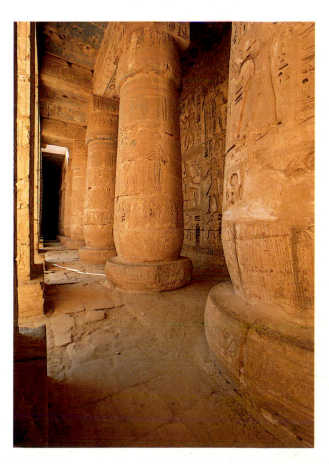

173

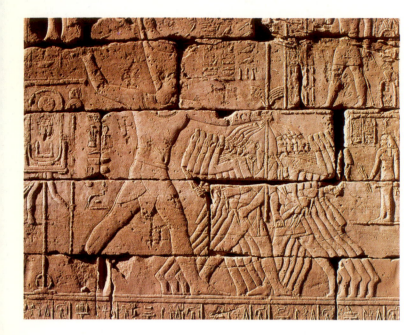

**Relief showing the pharaoh massacring his prisoners or cutting off their hands.**

The fallen enemy and the prisoners in these reliefs are so clearly depicted that they may be counted.

Opposite above:
The fortified High Gate–reminiscent of Canaanite towers–giving access to the temple of Medinet Habu in memory of the Egyptian victory.

Opposite below:
View of the lateral wall of the temple of Medinet Habu with the foundations of the Window of Appearances in the foreground. In the background, the cliffs of the Theban Hills.

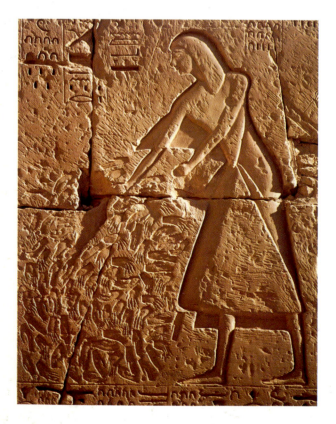

the chains of desert mountains, themselves a protective shield around the fertile valley of the Nile.

How did the royal city of Ramesses III transpose this concept into architectural terms? To comply with funerary rites, the temple precinct was reached from the Nile by means of a canal with landing wharves and piers. Viewed from the East, it appeared more like a fortress, with high crenellated stone walls and a battlemented gate, the Migdol Gateway. A low, outer mudbrick enclosure wall encircled the hallowed ground. Then, 33ft (10m) further toward the center rose an enormous wall 59ft (18m) high and 33ft (10m) thick enclosing an area with a perimeter of more than three quarters of a mile (320 x 220m). Inside this, a third, much lower boundary wall skirted the priests' dwellings, the administration buildings and the guard houses. Another rectangular mudbrick wall abutting the first pylon girdled a rectangular compound (558 x 427ft; 170 x 130m) inside which stood the royal palace, storerooms, and house of worship. Behind this wide pylon (246ft; 75m) lay a peristyle courtyard measuring 180 by 525ft (55 x 160m) ringed by a battered wall entirely built of stone and surmounted by a cavetto cornice. The core of the monument–the house of worship–was reached through a second pylon beyond which another courtyard led to the hypostyle hall before the inner sanctum, itself housed within a *naos* containing the Holy of Holies. In all, seven consecutive walls were raised to protect the idol.

The defensive character of the Divine City at Medinet Habu, necessitated perhaps by the resurgence of unrest along the borders, corresponded to a confirmation of pharaonic supremacy. The reliefs sculpted on the walls and pylons of the temple courtyards exalted military victories, depicted prisoners being executed, traitors punished, tongues and hands being cut off, portraits of the king himself crushing the skulls of his captives with his mace. The peaceful Egypt of the Old Kingdom slowly but surely became a despotic power. The Egyptian society eventually broke up into rival factions, and the Amun clergy of Upper Egypt progressively took power. Lower Egypt proclaimed its independence under the Twenty-first Dynasty (Tanite Period).

## The royal palaces

The royal palaces attached to the Ramesseum and others scattered about the Divine City at Medinet Habu of

**Architectural polychromy at Thebes.**

Great efforts were made in the 19th century to correctly represent ancient Egyptian art and architecture. The German archeologist Richard Lepsius has left us a good idea of the polychromy of the Ramesseum columns, and Jomard copied interesting graphic representations of the Mnemonium at Thebes. A group of scholars published the landmark *Description de l'Egypte* (1809), a record of the findings of the Bonaparte expedition of 1798, with detailed descriptions of the colors used in various pharaonic buildings.

Opposite:
This reconstitution, bearing the too-vague name of *Memnon*—which also applies to the colossi of King Amenophis II as well as the temple of King Sethos I at Abydos—shows the temple of Hathor at Deir el-Medina which dates from the Ptolemaic period. This interior view proves that the building had kept a good deal of its polychromy.

which limestone door jambs and other decorative vestiges remain, were small structures that served for the ritual of the Window of Appearances. The real residences of the kings in Thebes, Memphis, Per-Ramesses and other Egyptian cities were infinitely larger. As these palaces were constructed with less-permanent materials than tombs and temples, they have all disappeared, except for the reconstructions which archeologists have assembled from fragments. The foundations of the not very representative palace of King Akhenaten at Tell el-Amarna are the only remains of a royal residence that can be studied today.

The official buildings of the North Palace of Akhetaten were contained in a vast 1,350 square feet (125 square meter) area composed of a courtyard with porticos flanked on either side by a pair of long hypostyle halls each containing 36 columns (or 44 columns including those of the porticos).

Behind this section lay the Great Hall–a vast hypostyle hall totaling 310 columns and throne room–flanked by two hypostyle halls 52 columns each. This part of the palace alone counted no less than 584 columns.

The royal palace complex was in fact a miniature town accessed by a bridge spanning a principal avenue from where the king made his appearance; it was laid out on an orthogonal plan with a regularity seldom interrupted by random constructions. In addition to magnificent audience pavilions and reception areas devoted to ceremonies, there existed equally vast residential districts and storehouses. The private residence of the pharaoh comprised walled gardens, patios and waterworks stretching out among peristyle courtyards. One of the many squares may have contained a pool with a central islet devoted to a cosmological cult like the one described in the Osireion of Abydos.

This "Versailles" of the Egyptian sovereigns, spreading over an area of 12 or 13 acres (5 or 6ha), must have boasted a splendor that has probably never been equaled. The choice of mudbrick for its construction–possibly for temperature control–did not rule out embellishments in finer materials like white limestone, or alabaster, nor the presence of frescos or decorations in ceramic. The pharaoh must not have spared any expense in installing the extravagant waterworks, lush vegetation and flower beds we see depicted in the fragments of wall paintings scattered throughout the low and airy constructions.

**Woodwork from the Ramesside period.**

The tradition of wood sculpture was continued throughout the history of Egypt. This small polychrome *naos* with its two Hathoric columns at one side is decorated with a sacred barque. It was found at Deir el-Medina and must have held an idol for private devotional use. (Museo Egizio, Turin)

Opposite:
Detail from a wood statuette measuring approximately 23¹/₂in (60cm) and representing the insignia-bearer Penbui flanked by the gods Ptah and Amun. This piece dating from the Nineteenth Dynasty comes from the Drovetti collection. The face of this masterpiece is in the typical Ramesside style. (Museo Egizio, Turin)

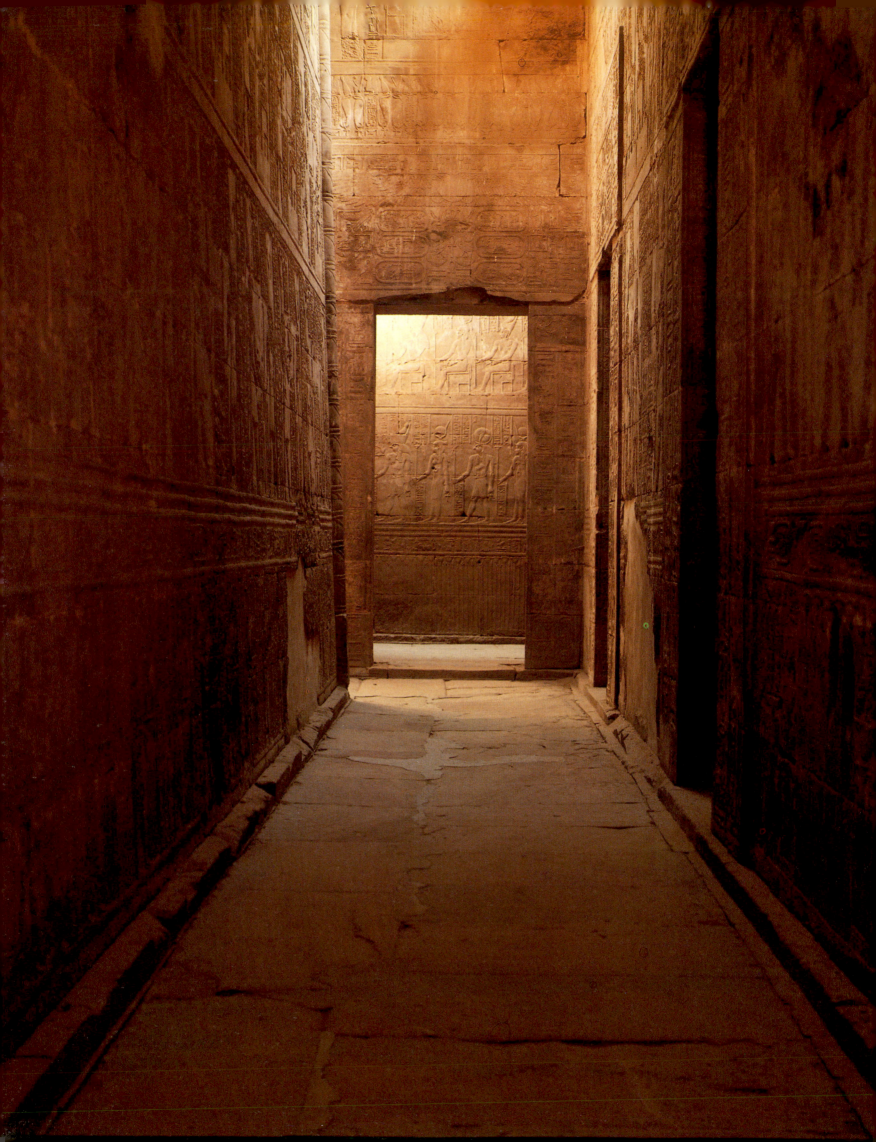

# Renaissance of architecture in Ptolemaic Egypt

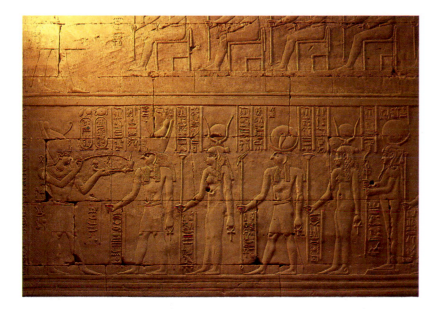

*Rows of Egyptian gods continued to decorate
the temples built by Upper-Egypt priests
during the Hellenistic Dynasties.*

Following the undistinguished reigns of the last Ramesside kings, Egypt fell prey once again to civil strife. This era marks the end of the New Kingdom and the beginning of the Third Intermediary Period. The city of Per-Ramesses to the east of the Delta was destroyed, and famine incited the population to revolt. The priests of the Amun temple at Thebes took power in Upper Egypt. A new family of sovereigns led by the self-proclaimed pharaoh Smendes, founded the Twenty-First Dynasty (*c.* 1085 BC) and ruled the new northern capital of Tanis. The Valley of the Nile was divided once again into two realms, and the region of Thebes was never again to regain its former glory.

The reign of Psusennes I (*c.* 1054 BC) at Tanis, however, was at the origin of a spectacular find made by the French

Opposite:

**Play of light and shadow in the mysterious corridor in the Horus Temple at Edfu.**

Paradoxically, never was such pharaonic architectural perfection attained as in the later temples built during the period of Greek domination. At the end of the corridor lies the chapel dedicated to Khons, god of the moon. The walls are decorated with cartouches of King Ptolemy III Evergetus who reigned in 246 BC and began the construction of the temple in 237 BC.

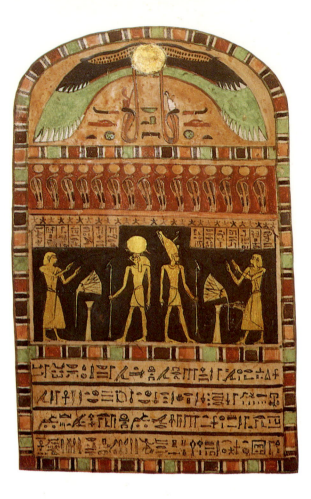

**Art of the Third Intermediate Period and objects in painted wood.**

Dating from the Twenty-Sixth Dynasty (c. 600 BC) this funerary stela in painted wood was discovered during Drovetti's excavations at Thebes. (Museo Egizio, Turin)

Opposite:
Detail of hieroglyph inscriptions in polychrome glass-paste encrusted in cedar wood. The writings reproduce chapter seventy-two of the *Book of the Dead* on the lid of the wood coffin of Djed Thod ef Ankh from Hermopolis Magna in Middle Egypt. This object of remarkable craftsmanship dates from the end of the fourth century BC.
(Museo Egizio, Turin)

Egyptologist Pierre Montet, whose digs were interrupted by the Second World War, but successfully resumed in 1945. The archeologist discovered a gold death mask and a hoard of fabulous jewelry in the sovereign's tomb.

The architecture of the Tanite Period was hardly brilliant judging from what remains. The master-builders contented themselves with raising enormous sanctuaries using building materials simply taken from the Ramesside temples.

## Foreign rule

The decline in pharaonic performance during the first millennium BC was checked and even reversed, with the arrival of Shoshenq, the great chief of a powerful Libyan tribe called the Ma. Ascending the Egyptian throne as Sesonchis I, he was able to reunite the Two Lands once again under his rule. His attack on the city of Jerusalem and pillage of the temple of Solomon (c. 925 BC) was one of Egypt's last military exploits on foreign soil.

The Egyptian pharaohs maintained their rank in spite of the growing importance of the clergy in the administration of the State. But in the 8th century BC, another break came about when the Nubians (the Sudanese populations of today) took advantage of certain signs of weakness and were able to annex the pharaonic lands to their own kingdom, thus founding a united territory from Meroe to the Delta region. This was the start of the Kushite monarchy (The territory of Kush was centered in Napata at the fourth cataract of the Nile.) and of a new empire (c. 715-664 BC).

Then, a great threat loomed from the Middle East with the Assyrian invasion of 671 BC, led by Esarhaddon, who took over the city of Memphis. After a short-lived respite when the Nubians returned to the throne, another Assyrian ruler, Assurbanipal, conquered the entire Valley of the Nile in 663 BC. The city of Thebes rose up against their new lords provoking the return to Middle Egypt of Assyrians troops which plundered the treasures accumulated over the centuries; temples and palaces were ravaged and the ancient capital fell into a hopeless decline which benefited only the Delta.

In 663 BC, the princes of Sais set up their capital at Memphis, founding the Twenty-Sixth Saite Dynasty under the sovereignty of Assyria. This lineage acquired real substance through a succession of strong kings beginning with Psammetichus I. An artistic revival took

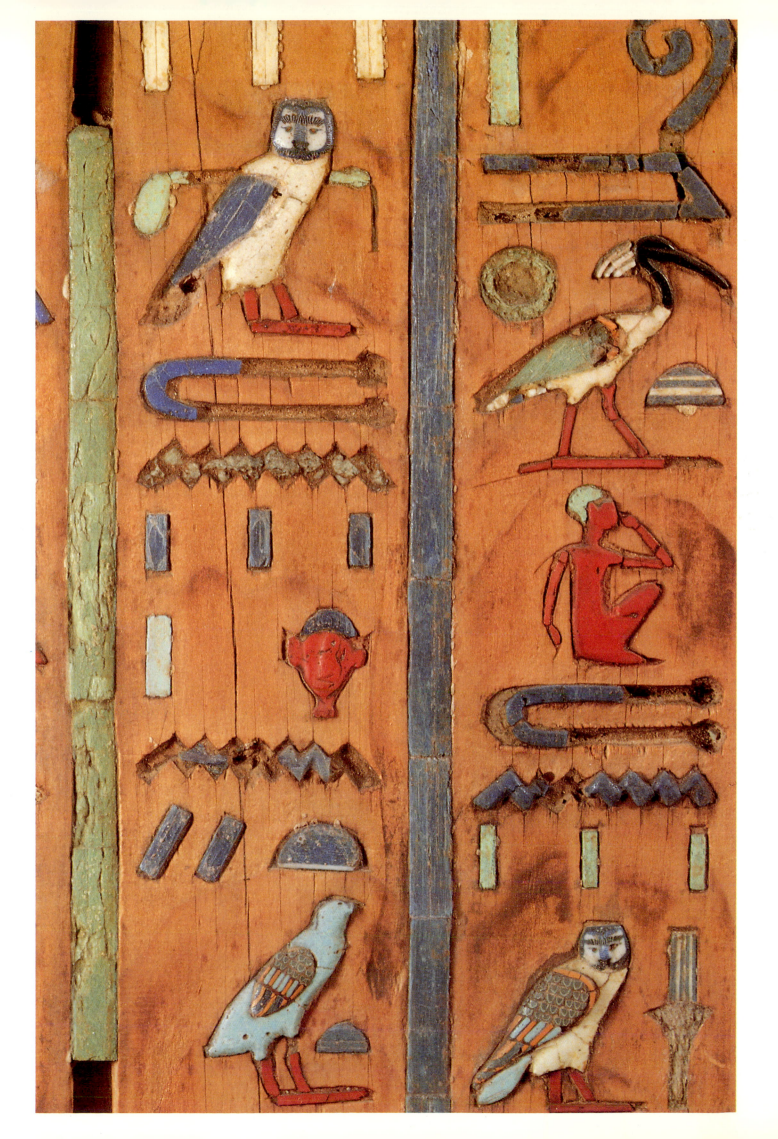

**The great pylon of the Horus Temple at Edfu.**

Begun under Ptolemy IX, around 110 BC, the temple, whose decoration
was not finished before 45 BC, is of massive height with a lower middle
part pierced by a gateway. The edifice reaches a height of 118 ft
(36 m)–equivalent to a 12-story building–and a width of 230 ft (70 m).
The four vertical niches on the façade once served to rig huge poles from
which banners were flown.

place characterized essentially by a return to ancient traditions. The former administrative and religious division of the territory into nomes was reinstated, and the digging of the canal linking the Nile to the Red Sea was resumed. Egypt seemed to have risen from its ashes. Saite art took inspiration from models of the Old Kingdom, creating a renaissance that would last until 550 BC.

What peace there was, however, was only relative. The Assyrians aggressors were replaced by the Babylonians who, although they never succeeded in occupying any part of the Valley, remained a constant threat until they were overshadowed in turn by the growing might of the Persians led by King Cambyses who conquered Egypt (525 BC) and founded the Twenty-Seventh Dynasty. Darius I occupied the throne and was followed by Xerxes and Artaxerxes. A revolt in 404 BC gave Egypt back its independence and the country was governed briefly by the Twenty-Eighth Saite Dynasty. A Twenty-Ninth Dynasty of princes from Mendes was rapidly followed by a Thirtieth which was distinguished by the rule of King Nectanebo I who was the most distinguished ruler. He capitulated in 342 BC to Artaxerxes III, whose army returned to Persia taking with it the Egyptian's sacred books and many statues of their gods as booty.

Under Darius III mighty Persia fell to Alexander and his Greek armies. Other triumphs of the great King of Macedon included the battle of Issos in 333 BC, the sieges of Tyre and Gaza, the entry into the Nile Delta in 332 BC, and the founding of the city of Alexandria. Upon the death of Alexander in 323 BC, Ptolemy, the son of a distinguished general in Alexander's army was appointed governor *(satrap)* of the province of the Nile Valley, and when the unity of the Macedonian empire was broken, Ptolemy declared himself King of Egypt.

The presence of the Ptolemies marked the beginning of an Egypto-Greek culture in the Delta. In Upper Egypt, neither the appearance of Hellenistic nor subsequent Roman kings on the throne of the pharaohs were to modify the indigenous characteristics of the architecture that emerged during the last 500 years of decline of the Egyptian civilization. No influence of Greek art is perceptible in the temples that were erected by the master-builders of the Ptolemaic and Roman eras.

In the face of foreign domination, the Egyptians turned to time-tested practices that they had learned through the centuries. Faithful to traditions, respectful of their heritage, they resisted change with xenophobic ardor and

**Religious observance of Egypt's latest period were haunted by the gods of salvation: Isis and Osiris.**

This lovely basalt statue from the tomb of Psamtek–chief of the royal scribes–in Saqqara represents the goddess Isis and dates from the Twenty-Sixth Dynasty.

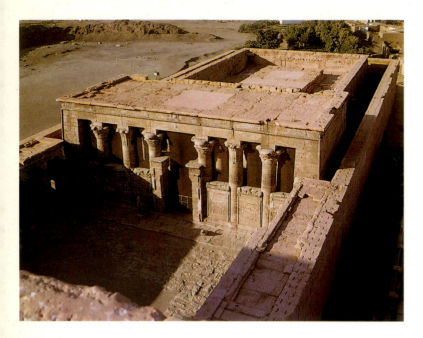

**Architectural perfection during the reign of the Ptolemies.**

From the summit of the pylon, the entire temple dedicated to Horus at Edfu is built like a fortress surrounded by high walls. The hypostyle hall is visible through the courtyard and, farther on, the sanctuary bordered by a corridor.

Below:
The airy portico of the courtyard at Edfu.

Opposite:
The high columns of the portico with their composite capitals precede the hypostyle hall. Sculpted on the pillars are decorative scenes of gods to whom the Macedonian sovereigns rendered homage with offerings.

rose against their conquerors under native rulers whenever the opportunity presented itself. It is surprising, however, after a lapse of time covering one thousand years of uninterrupted foreign hegemony exercised by Libyan and Nubian usurpers, Assyrian and Persian kings and Greco-Roman rulers, that Egypt, in its twilight years, was able to maintain its own forms and styles and continue to produce some of the most perfect examples of its traditional architecture.

### The great temples of the Late Age

Reliefs, stelae and statuary are the only remaining vestiges of the Saite monuments (7th and 6th centuries BC). The building materials of certain temples of Lower Egypt were re-employed for Greek constructions in Alexandria and many sanctuaries were destroyed by Arab limeburners for the manufacture of lime. From the Persian period (c. 524-404 BC), vestiges from the Hibis temple (oasis of Khargeh) evolved toward a definite style that would dominate under the Ptolemaic reigns. Three centuries of a more stable rule by the Ptolemies (also called the Lagide lineage, for it was founded by Ptolemy, son of Lagus) in Upper Egypt offered some respite after years of upheaval. During this period only occasional peasant uprisings against excessive taxes interrupted the building campaigns which produced immense temples and other constructions. Ptolemaic art expressed itself in more than a hundred sites.

The five great sacred complexes that have survived until today, most of them in a remarkable state of conservation, are Edfu, Dendera, Kom Ombo, Esna, and Philae. Some of these were built or completed during the Roman period. The magnificent hypostyle hall of Esna was entirely constructed after the birth of Christ.

These sanctuaries which were devoted to the ruler, whose names are carved in hieroglyphic cartouches on the pillars and walls, were Greek or Roman: Ptolemy, Cleopatra, Nero, Trajan, and Decius. By taking allegiance with a foreign power yet maintaining the belief of a deified sovereign, the priests of Upper Egypt not only obtained the right to perpetuate the rites of ancient Egypt but to conserve the principle of a pharaoh-god, master of pharaonic religion and its sacred architecture since 3000 BC.

The remarks previously made concerning New Kingdom temples like Medinet Habu (built under Ramesses III), whose relatively good state of conservation

has allowed us to discover the architect's plan and layout, also hold true for monuments like the great temple of Horus at Edfu. Here, as well as at the temple of Hathor at Dendera, which was built on a similar plan, the roof slabs have remained intact giving us an idea of the role played by light in the course of the different phases of the cult. Here, we can go from the vestibule *(pronaos)*, fully bathed in light, to the dark depths of the inner sanctum and plunged into an atmosphere of mysticism and contemplation.

The complementary nature of Edfu and Dendera is not due to chance. Both sanctuaries were devoted to the cult of Horus, the sun falcon, son of Isis and Osiris, and–in this particular version of the legend–the husband of Hathor, goddess of beauty, joy and love, represented by a sacred cow. Many feasts took place with processions and navigation on the Nile between the two shrines. During the festivities, the statue of one of the temples would be brought to visit the other.

### Architectural details

The great Temple of Horus at Edfu, the most complete and best-conserved sanctuary in Egypt, is also the best documented thanks to the numerous texts and descriptive scenes carved on its walls. The construction and decoration of the temple took a total of 180 years to complete (*c.* 237-57 BC). Built on a gigantic scale, the monument covers 75,000 square feet (7000 square meters); its massive pylon measures 259ft (79m) wide and 115ft (35m) high. The great gateway is crowned with a cavetto cornice adorned by a winged disc–the symbol of Horus and leads into a vast peristyle courtyard surrounded on three sides by a portico supported by 32 columns with highly-decorated capitals, symmetrically arranged in pairs. The fourth side with 6 high shafts forms the vestibule *(pronaos)*. Its gateway was flanked by an huge pair of granite falcons, one of which is intact. Small rooms were built against the courtyard wall on either side of the entranceway; the one on the left contained the canopic jars and the one on the right served as a temple library. The outstanding feature of the peristyle courtyard however was the stunning series of reliefs depicting the temple ceremonies. Doorways on either side led into an open-roofed ambulatory running between the sides of the temple and its inner enclosure wall. The following room, the great hypostyle hall, was

**Horus, the sky god represented by a falcon.**

A free-standing statue of the bird of prey, equated with the king, wearing the double royal crown reigns in front of the Edfu temple's façade. This hieratic granite sculpture attests to the vitality of pharaonic art throughout the Ptolemaic Dynasty, which immediately preceded the Christian era.

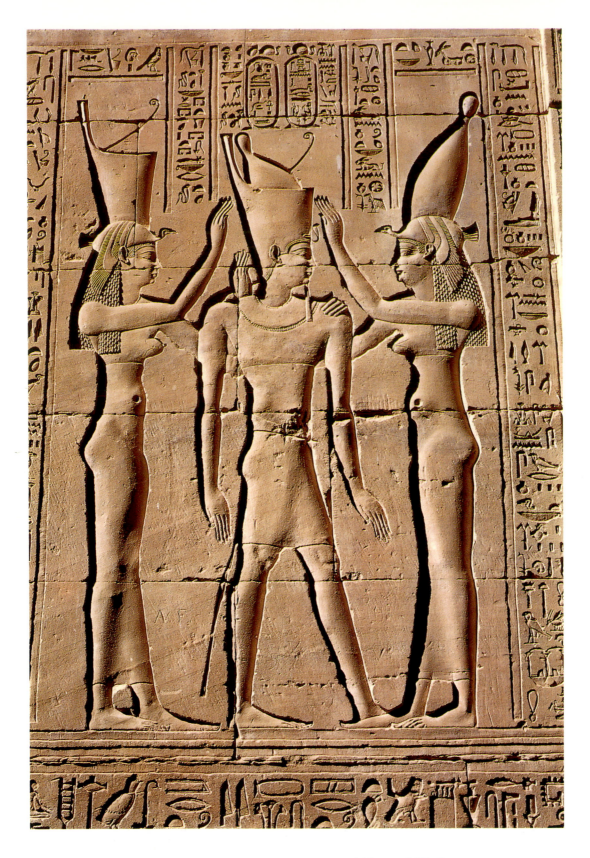

**The pharaoh crowned by the goddesses Nekhbet and Wadjet, symbols of Upper and Lower Egypt.**

Of the many reliefs in the corridor at Edfu, this scene is the most famous. Sculpted during the reign of Ptolemy VI (181-145 BC), it depicts two female divinities combining their insignia and crowning the pharaoh with the *pschent*, or double crown, which they are blessing with their elongated hands.

Opposite:
Detail of Wadjet wearing the vulture headdress. The sculpture adds a certain sensuality to the graceful relief.

**The first and second hypostyle halls at Edfu.**

Although the first hall of the Temple of Horus, with its eighteen great columns supporting roof slabs 50 ft (15 m) above the floor, is fairly well lit, the second, seen from the Offering Chamber near the entrance, lies in the shadows. The darkness is only partially relieved at certain spots. Over all the surfaces–both walls and pillars–a myriad of reliefs animate the rigorous yet serene architecture, well suited to devotion.

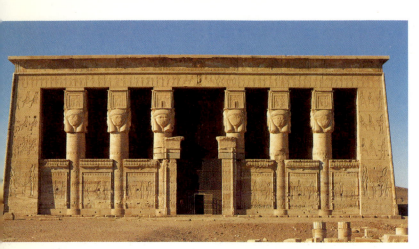

**Denera, dedicated to the goddess Hathor, is modeled on the Edfu temple.**

The plan of Dendera resembles that of Edfu. Begun toward 80 BC under King Ptolemy XII, the building does not have a pylon and has lost its surrounding wall. The monumental façade of the hypostyle hall is decorated with Hathoric capitals bearing effigies of the sistrum-headed goddess above low walls on each side of the broken-lintel gateway.

Below:
The first hypostyle hall of the Dendera temple was built toward AD 35 during the reign of the Roman emperor Caligula.

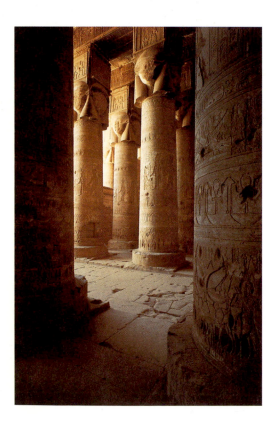

built with a screen-wall (a technique already mentioned in connection with the White Chapel of King Sesostris I at Karnak from the Middle Kingdom) culminating at 52ft (16m). The hall contained 18 enormous shafts surmounted by palm, floral and composite capitals (more complex than those of the New Kingdom).

Behind, shrouded in a dark area, lay a second smaller and lower hypostyle hall supported by 4 rows of 12 columns. This space lit from square wells cut in the ceiling slabs enveloped the room in a profoundly pious, almost dramatic atmosphere. The roof openings acted like spotlights from which rays of light streamed through the dark.

Further along stood the Room of the Offerings from which a winding staircase ascended, in darkness, to the roof of the building, and from there, another staircase led back down to the temple. The right way round the temple was indicated on the reliefs which depicted priests and gods climbing the winding flights of stairs, landing after landing, and then taking the other straight staircase down from the roof, step by step, as if the procession were descending into a rock-cut tomb *(hypogeum)*. These stairs were used during the New Year's ceremonies when the priests carried the divine statues into the sunlight so that the union with the solar disc could take place and the idols could recover their vigor and efficiency.

The next area, called the Room of the Associated Gods, led to a complex system of peripheral chapels giving onto the Corridor of Mysteries; this corridor encircled only the shrine, but unlike the ambulatory walk, was covered with roof slabs and lay entirely in shadow.

Representing stations of transition or transformation, all of the entranceways held a very special religious significance. They had heavy doors sheathed in bronze or silver and encrusted with precious stones and were only unsealed for the great rituals. The daily activities of the temple such as offerings, sacrifices and daily prayers were carried on through secondary openings and narrow passages allowing the priests to go about their duties.

The whole layout was focused however on the small dark womb-like envelope, the Holy of Holies. This ultimate envelope consisted of a free-standing, battered tabernacle adorned with a torus molding whose empty granite *naos* housed the divine image inhabited by the "living god." It had no windows or openings for light to enter, and a gilded wooden canopy was probably hung over it as added protection. In front of the tabernacle

**The fifty-six-foot bulk of the heavy Hathoric columns in the Dendera temple.**

Pillars covered with reliefs support the architraves and roof slabs. The scenes represent great processions of gods and goddesses in their barques as well as the mysteries of the sacred zodiac.

**The lighting technique in the late sanctuaries.**

The Ptolemaic and Roman temples in pharaonic Egypt have often conserved their roofs permitting us to discover the way in which the architects attended to the lighting.

Opposite:
The sanctuary encircled by a mysterious corridor in the center of the Dendera temple. Light-wells cut into the ceiling and openings at the top of walls–some vertical some horizontal and more or less splayed–provide very low-angled lighting on the starred ceilings and architectonic volumes.

Above:
View through the most sacred part of the temple–the Holy of Holies–with a perspective of the succession of chapels. In the foreground, an altar for offerings, and, on the right glowing in the shadows, the torus molding of the black granite *naos* of Nectanebo II, dated 350 BC.

rested the plinth of Horus' sacred barque. The statue of the divinity was placed inside the barque's cabin, and paraded on a handbarrow carried on the priests' shoulders during processions on certain feast days and was even taken to visit other sanctuaries.

## The principles of architecture

The ground level of the temple continued to rise, for each room was placed on a slightly higher level than the last, while the ceilings became lower and the light dimmed. At the highest point, the inner sanctum lay in almost total darkness. As for the crypts housing the precious instruments of the cult, they were embedded in the thickness of the walls and lay in pitch dark.

Another observation should be made concerning the different enclosures, one inside the other, forming protective layers around the idol (already mentioned with regard to the Ramessides temples): the external face of each of these envelopes was battered and crowned with cavetto cornices and torus moldings giving the "impression of a blockhouse" (J.-L. de Cénival) and turning the pharaonic temple into a true sacred fortress.

All of these architectural feats were enhanced by the exceptional quality of the building materials and workmanship. None of the Ptolemaic temples gave the impression that hastiness or the difficulty of handling such volume led to incomplete or badly constructed monuments, as was unfortunately the case in some of the great sanctuaries of the Ramessides. On the contrary, during the last centuries of the Egyptian civilization, the pharaonic master-builders seemed determined to achieve the quintessence of an architecture built for eternity.

## The City of God

The temple formed the hub of a great cluster of buildings inside a vast, self-sufficient domain composed of agricultural estates on which the inhabitants of many villages worked. Many of the larger temples possessed a sacred lake, a large rectangular pool (vestiges of which may be seen in Dendera) where the priests would undertake purification rites; it was also used for rituals involving the sacred barque. Temples built along the Nile featured a nilometer–steps leading down to the river to measure the water level–which served to calculate taxes. As the land surrounding these temples has not been

198

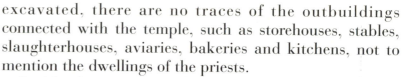

excavated, there are no traces of the outbuildings connected with the temple, such as storehouses, stables, slaughterhouses, aviaries, bakeries and kitchens, not to mention the dwellings of the priests.

Inside the temple enclosure stood an independent construction, the solar kiosk, used for the ritual presentation of the divine statues to the rays of the sun. This small structure was sometimes accompanied by an astronomical chapel, like the one for the zodiac at Dendera. In front of the temple stood the birth house *(mammisi)* of the pharaoh-god–a small sanctuary devoted to the cult of the deified king. In addition, many areas around the temple were set aside for special functions, such as the Hall of the Treasures, the library housing the sacred texts on cosmology and mythology, the laboratory of perfumes and fumigations, the holy sacristy, and various chapels devoted to complementary divinities.

The precinct–temple, annexes and sacred lake represented a "city of god," a city within the real city, with officials, shopkeepers, craftsmen, servants, boatmen, artists, landowners, and soldiers in garrison. A royal administration levied taxes on the whole domain, but another body under the authority of the clergy supervised the cult and the financing of the construction and upkeep of the temples and tombs, often funded by endowments set up by the faithful. The importance of this group of religious officials was considerable, as it presided over the immense undertakings of the architects, stone cutters, masons, sculptors and painters.

**The artist Domenico Valeriano found inspiration in drawings made by Vivant Denon, a member of Bonaparte's Egyptian Campaign in 1798, to illustrate a book by Girolamo Segato published in Florence in 1835.**

The reproduction of one of the Hathoric columns (opposite) in the hypostyle hall and the ceiling slab with a representation of the zodiac (the original is on display at the Louvre Museum) attest to the extraordinary polychrome decoration of the buildings. It was found over a chapel on the terrace of the Temple of Hathor and used in the New Year Festival.

201

# PHILAE AND THE LATE TEMPLES

## THE LATE SURGE
## OF EGYPTIAN ART

*Philae saved from submersion: the "Pearl of Egypt"*
*was transported, stone by stone, above the high-water*
*level of the Nile.*

In the Roman period during the initial spread of Christianity, building campaigns continued unabated in Upper Egypt. The temples of Dendera, Kom Ombo and Philae were completed and the last touches were added to the enormous temple of Esna, of which only the large hypostyle hall remains intact.

The Ptolemaic style, maintained throughout the Roman period, did not become stereotyped. Each temple erected during these four or five centuries showed interesting variations. Thus, contrary to Edfu, the first hypostyle hall of Dendera, built during the reigns of Caligula and Claudius, did not bear classic columns but enormous shapeless cylindrical shafts surmounted by four-sided capitals sculpted with representations of the

Opposite:

**The silhouette of the beautiful goddess Hathor, sculpted during the time of Ptolemy XII-Neos Dionysos (c. 80 BC), decorates the first pylon of the Philae temple.**

This representation of the goddess, considered too sensual by the Copts, was covered with plaster when the sanctuary became a church, and Christian monks inscribed texts in Greek characters on the flat outer surfaces of the sunk relief. The body of the goddess however was restored to its former glory when the plaster fell off the wall; only the head had been defaced.

cow-eared face of the goddess Hathor. Above each head was a large dice-shaped bearing-slab carved with a rattle-like musical instrument (*sistrum*), the cult symbol of Hathor. Unfortunately, these sculptures were defaced during the iconoclastic campaigns of the early Christians.

The formula of Hathoric columns had already been employed, but with less success from an aesthetic point of view, in another hypostyle hall of the Dendera temple: the Hall of Appearances. Here, the shafts of the columns supported not only the cube-shaped capital and the bearing-slab, but a composite floral capital as well. The three-storied capitals perched on top of shafts gave the building an ugly baroque appearance, for the height of the capital together with the architrave was equal to the height of the shaft alone. In this instance, the master-builders gave preference to religious significance instead of taking a coherent architectural design into account. Thus, we can assume that the hall, constructed a century later, corrected this aesthetic problem.

We should also mention that the Dendera temple never had a pylon and that it lost its high wall when the Copts re-employed the stones to construct a church nearby. Inside the mudbrick temple enclosure measuring 853 by 918ft (260 x 280m) lay several smaller edifices, including the Mammisi of Nectanebo, a Roman birth house devoted to the birth of Isis, as well as a sanitarium created for the sick who came there to seek favor from Hathor, to whom they attributed certain healing powers.

## The Temple of Kom Ombo

Another example of the particularities of each temple was the sanctuary of Kom Ombo dedicated to two gods, Sobek, the crocodile-headed god, and Horus the elder, which crowned the promontory overlooking the Nile. While the majority of cult chambers at Kom Ombo were shared by the two deities, each had his own shrine and processional way. The temple had two enclosures forming an inner and an outer ambulatory around the shrine area. The outer ambulatory was set aside for the faithful who flocked to the temple to honor their gods.

This monument, undertaken at the beginning of the 2nd century BC, dominated a magnificent site high above the eastern bank of the Nile. Its first hypostyle hall dated from 164 BC and its courtyard was erected in honor of Tiberius; the decoration of the sanctuary continued up to the time of Vespasian and the complex was finally completed under

**The Great Temple of Isis at Philae relocated on Agilkia Island.**

Between the temple's two pylons, entirely reconstructed in its original building materials on the new site in 1972, is the great courtyard bordered to the west by a *mammisi*, or birth house. This is where the mysteries of the divine birth of the sovereign were played out. The Hathoric columns support four-sided *sistrum*-capitals bearing the features of the cow-eared goddess Hathor.

**The Temple of Philae was given an important place in the *Description de l'Egypte*.**

The scholars of the scientific Bonaparte expedition were impressed by the superb polychromy inside the temple.

Above:
A highly colorful representation of the god Amun-Re seated on his throne.

Opposite above:
These were the lovely colors that could be seen in the hypostyle hall in 1800 before the first Aswan Dam–completed in 1902–condemned the rooms to partial submersion.

Opposite below:
The antique interpretation of a pharaoh wearing a composite crown, rendering homage to the goddess Maat, whose headdress bears the ostrich plume, and Sekhmet (?) the lioness-headed goddess.

Macrinus in the 3rd century AD. Now that most of the outside walls have disappeared, sunlight casts shadows on the ruined halls and penetrates into the heart of the temple allowing us to enjoy the remarkable quality of the decoration. The most interesting reliefs are preserved on a rear wall and, at eye level, the figures of two goddesses seated on birth stools may be seen.

### The Temple of Philae

The temple of Isis of Philae south of Aswan was dismantled stone by stone and transported to higher ground between 1972 and 1980 thanks to international efforts. The sanctuary, now situated on a granite isle above the first cataract, was begun at the time of Ptolemy II-Philadelphus and decorated, for the most part, under Ptolemy XII-Neos Dionysos. The complex, laid out along a bent axis probably resulting from lack of space, was composed of a great entrance colonnade, two pylons between which lay the superb birth house surrounded by Hathoric columns completed under Tiberius and the magnificent Kiosk of Trajan. Philae, unlike most of the major temples of Egypt, does not appear to have been built over an older sanctuary, for the earliest vestiges discovered there date from the Twenty-Fifth Dynasty. Devoted to the cult of Isis, the goddess of salvation, it was Egypt's last functioning temple and housed the last priests able to read hieroglyphs and write with them in the *demotic* style until it was closed down by Justinian in AD 551.

### The decoration of late temples

The Ptolemaic and Roman temples of Upper Egypt with their careful attention to detail, superb craftsmanship, noble proportions, intricate composite capitals, and liberal use of hard stones exhibited a solemn grace, although much of their relief, sculpture and painting did not have the purity of those of the Old Kingdom and some of the hieroglyphs were coarse. However, these monuments magnificently summed up a 3000-year civilization and served as the hallmark of a culture and its artistic standards.

The great mythological scenes that covered the walls of Edfu, Dendera and Philae tempered classicism with a touch of sensuality. Lovely goddesses, their long and fine silhouettes wrapped in close-fitting garments, their breasts high and proud, bore the signs of a certain

206

**The splendor of the Temple of Isis at Philae.**

In spite of its late construction–the time of the Greco-Roman occupation–the insular ensemble of Philae displays a real beauty. This is illustrated as much by the face of the goddess emerging from the lotus bud on the lovely Hathoric capitals as in the architectural constructions.

humanization. An entire mythology with its actors and magic signs, and a whole bestiary animated the buildings. Each wall, each column, each lintel, each roof slab was decorated with a multitude of sculptures treated in raised or in sunk relief, expressing a profound piety. Great blocks of sculpted sandstone were painted over a fine layer of stucco. Colors and polished surfaces must have shone brightly in the hypostyle halls and more subtly in inner chambers, such as the Room of the Electrum whose reliefs were entirely covered with a natural pale yellow alloy of gold and silver.

Everywhere, reliefs covered the walls harmoniously blending hieroglyphs of the sacred texts with scenes of sovereigns making sacrifices to the gods; the ceilings displayed representations in relief of the firmament or of the zodiac; beams of light from the roof wells played on statues of Horus the falcon-headed god, or Osiris, the creator of the earth, lying on his funerary bed; many other divinities slept for eternity in the shadows of the crypts.

## Canon codes for the clergy

Each sanctuary had thousands of texts carved on its walls in increasingly more complex hieroglyphic writing composed of two thousand signs, instead of the four hundred used in the New Kingdom, and required the intervention of specialists to decipher them. An interesting point regarding these texts and scenes of the late temples is that they issued instructions on how to follow the cult, with detailed reminders for the priests describing each phase of the ritual. They indicated not only the words to be pronounced, but the movements and even the dances accompanied by musical instruments to be carried out by the clergy during the great feasts.

Thus, in the vast hypostyle hall of Esna, studied by Serge Sauneron, the following orders were given: "Pronounce: Day of Rejoicing, the gods are joyful, the men are elated, for the floods have arrived." The text then read: "Dance in honor of god, in honor of the son of Re, the eternal Pharaoh." And the reliefs depicted Trajan dancing. In the same manner for the ritual of the union of the disc, the texts pointed out the gestures to be accomplished and the hymns to be sung: "Purify yourself, do not commit reprehensible acts." The text continued : "Return to the first hypostyle hall. Unite with the Disc, then proceed to the Hall of the Appearances." Each ritual was thus strictly defined leaving nothing to improvisation, ensuring that "the texts be followed," and according to the existence of a punctilious and immemorial liturgy to which one had to conform. The most astounding aspect of these great hymns, whose verses ran along the columns of the temple, was the profound lyricism of the words and their sacred message.

The following hymn to Isis demonstrates the scope of the sacred literature of Late Egypt:

> *O Isis, great Goddess, Mother of god, Originator of Life, you reign over Philae and over the forbidden land.*
> *O Sovereign of the Isles, mourning Goddess, you reconstitute the body of your brother Osiris.*
> *O great and powerful Sovereign of the Gods, the Goddesses praise your name.*
> *O beneficent Magician, you chase away the devil with utterances falling from your lips.*
> *O mighty Goddess, most powerful, great in the Sky, rule over the Celestial Bodies and give the Stars their place.*
> *O Isis, Originator of Life, Queen of Philae and Queen of the southern deserts.*

Thanks to the decipherment of the sacred texts we have been able to gain a better knowledge of the rites carried on within the walls of the temples of ancient Egypt. Without this information the great monuments of the Valley of the Nile would be nothing but meaningless ruins. These texts prove that the design of the temples had less to do with the whims of the pharaonic master-builders than to their piety. These magnificent spaces, illuminated by the human spirit and subtly and rhythmically designed found their purpose in a religious vision which has marked them for all time.

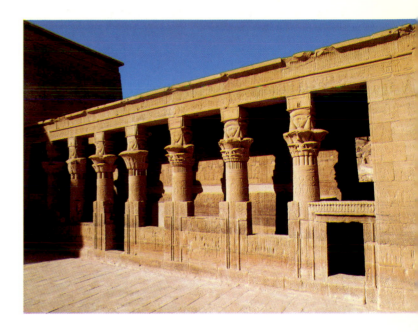

**A great variety of structural supports during the Late Period.**

At the time of Augustus and Tiberius, supporting pillars became very diversified, as we can see from in the Mammisi of Philae and the great gateway at the edge of the island, with its composite capitals and double-pedestal.

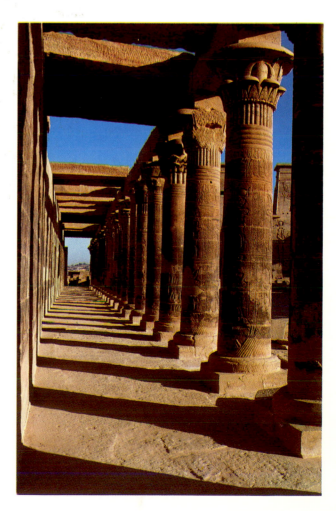

209

# Conclusion

*Richard Lepsius traveled as far as Gebel Barkal
near Napata in Upper Nubia to copy the paintings
in the temples built under the Nubian King Taharqa.
(7th century BC)*

This brief account retraces the exceptional achievements of Egypt's master-builders which have drawn unfailing admiration since Antiquity. These architectural masterpieces, erected over a period of more than three thousand years throughout more than a score of dynasties, suffered much injury during their long history—some being damaged beyond repair by the passage of time, others modified by ambitious rulers or destroyed by hate and pillaged by the greed of their enemies. Many have been resuscitated, excavated, salvaged, relocated, and rebuilt with loving care. Archeologists, art historians, artists, photographers, archivists, architects, engineers, anthropologists, and scholars have assisted Egyptologists in acquiring and

Opposite:

**Never completed, the immense elegant Kiosk of Trajan is the swan-song of Egyptian architecture.**

Here, in solemn magnificence, ends the three-thousand-year evolution of the science devoted to Egyptian cults by the Pharaonic master-builders. Here, too, modern technology has contributed to saving from submersion this testimonial of a civilization whose achievements remain unsurpassed.

211

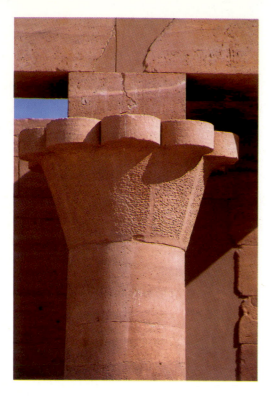

**These ultimate Egyptian creations seem unfinished and hyperthrophic.**

Above:
At Philae, one of the capitals of the west colonnade was first merely roughed out while awaiting the sculptor's chisel.

Opposite:
The great hypostyle hall at Esna, built between AD 41 and 79, under the reigns of the Roman emperors from Claudius to Titus, remains intact but the temple that once existed behind the hall has entirely disappeared. In studying Segato's colored engraving (1836) based on earlier drawings by Vivant Denon, great differences appear. Clearly, Segato's treatment of the engaged columns between the screen walls and the painting is an imaginary reconstitution.

accumulating an enormous sum of knowledge to better understand these monuments of the past.

The ancient Egyptian master-builders devised an incomparable synthesis of art forms. Statues, reliefs, and wall paintings constituted an integral part of their buildings. Furthermore, the rituals and the ceremonies that took place in the sacred halls could not be separated from the structures which had been designed for them, as we have seen earlier in this book.

Indeed, there are few examples of such stylistic unity elsewhere. Neither Mesopotamia, whose constructions were mostly made of brick and of which few vestiges remain, nor India, whose productions were of a much later date, nor Pre-Columbian America, where the megalithic sanctuaries of the Incas from the 15th century only counted a half a dozen sites, nor Ancient Greece, whose temples were smaller structures, express the unique, awesome splendor of the pharaonic buildings. Perhaps only early Roman architecture, or in an entirely different context the Romanesque and Gothic churches built many centuries later, can counterbalance the preeminence of Egyptian architecture, although being diametrically opposite modes of expression. Moreover, many later cultures borrowed architectural principles and expressions from Egypt. In Achaemenian Persia, cavetto cornices surmounted doors; in Greece, the Doric style developed from Egypt's fluted columns; in Rome, basilicas with forests of columns were actually hypostyle halls.

Pharaonic architecture astonishes us with its spontaneity, clarity of design and legibility of volumes. Such simplicity could only be attained through a experienced handling of geometrical concepts. The design of the pyramids was based on squares and the isosceles triangle, the mastabas on trapezes, the pillars and lintels on parallelepipeds, and the columns on cylinders.

Even the cosmological hymns written in hieroglyphs expressed this profound respect for geometry. Carved on the walls of the Esna Temple is a poem dedicated to Khnum, the god of creation, who fashioned the body of a child on a potter's wheel and implanted him as a seed in his mother's womb. This unknown poet displayed a deep understanding of the rigorous system that commanded the Egyptian world and, voiced in these words the wishes of the young king who ruled at the time:

*May he give you the South as far as the wind blows,*
*the North as far as the sea rolls,*
*the East as far as the sun rises,*

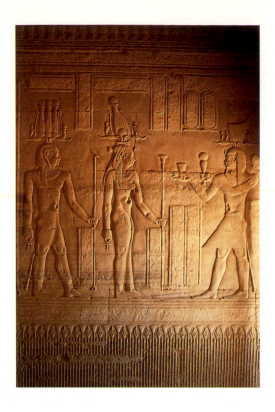

**The artists' activities appear to have been interrupted in the middle of their execution.**

The end of Egyptian art and architecture is not marked by a slow death or withering, but by a sudden and devastating collapse. In the chapels of the temple of Kom Ombo erected during the reign of Macrinus (3rd century AD), the figures on the reliefs are sculpted with care but the spaces provided for the hieroglyphs remained blank.

Opposite:
At Dendera, the superb mammisi from the Roman era illustrates the divine birth and suckling of the royal infant. Were the great scenes sculpted between AD 100 and 140 on the screen walls about Trajan's, Hadrian's or Antoninus Pius' mythical childhood? One thing is sure, the depictions are not decadent, but, on the contrary, vigorous confirmations of Egypt's struggle against the rise of new religions.

*the West as far as he sets.*
*May he come like the floods*
*to feed the Two Lands,*
*to give life to all creatures.*
*May he purvey the products of all regions*
*embraced by the sun between the four*
*Supporters of Heaven.*

The earth as seen by the ancient Egyptians was held up by the four Supporters of Heaven aligned precisely along the north/south and east/west axes. The pharaonic master-builders transposed to their architectural designs this cosmic image in which the earth was seen as held up by four pillars. The profound spirituality that emerges from ancient Egyptian buildings also emanates from certain construction techniques. During a dig, archeologists discovered the foundations of a temple whose stone blocks had been carefully disposed under the angle of a wall in the exact same spot that they had occupied in an older sanctuary, as attested by the inscriptions still visible on one of the blocks. In the mind of the ancient Egyptians architects, each block not only performed an architectonic function but acquired certain spiritual attributes that would remain forever. A stone block thus became a seed which would germinate in a new construction, bringing a timelessness to the building process, in the same way that the gods of the Egyptian pantheon underwent a process of regeneration that brought permanence to the world itself.

In Egyptian architecture rocks carved of granite, lime-stone, sandstone, and schist precisely and perfectly adjusted, found their place in a gigantic puzzle that associated the material and the immaterial dimensions of space, light, and spirit.

This is the message of the pharaonic master-builders.

**Ramesses II seated on the throne**

Polychrome relief from Abu Simbel copied by Rosellini.

# Bibliography

ALDRED, Cyril, *Egyptian Art in the Days of the Pharaohs*, London: Thames & Hudson, 1980, and New York: Thames & Hudson, 1985.

CÉNIVAL, Jean-Louis de, *Egypte, époque pharaonique*, *Architecture universelle* series, photographs by Henri Stierlin. Fribourg: 1964.

DAUMAS, François, *La civilisation de l'Egypte pharaonique*, Paris: 1965.

DONADONI ROVERI, Anna Maria, *La civilisation des Egyptiens*, Vol. I: *La vie quotidienne*; Vol. II: *Les croyances religieuses*; Vol. III: *Les arts de la célébration*. Milan: Museo Egizio, Torino, 1988-1989.

EDWARDS, I.E.S., *Pyramids of Egypt*, London & New York: 1961; revised, Penguin, 1985.

HOBSON, Christine, *Exploring the World of the Pharaohs*, London: Thames & Hudson, 1987.

JENKINS, Nancy, *The Boat beneath the Pyramid, King Cheops' Royal Ship*, London: Thames & Hudson 1980, and New York: Holt, Rinehart & Winston, 1980.

LAUER, Jean-Philippe, *Histoire monumentale des pyramides d'Egypte*, Vol. I. Cairo: 1962.

LAUER, Jean-Philippe, *Saqqara, the Royal Cemetery of Memphis*, London: Thames & Hudson 1976, and New York: Scribner's, 1976.

LECLANT, Jean (ed.), *Le monde égyptien, les pharaons, L'univers des formes* series. Vol. I, *Le temps des pyramides*, Chap. III: Architecture, by Jean-Philippe Lauer; Vol. II: *L'empire des conquérants*, Chap. I: Architecture, by Paul Barguet; Vol.III, *L'Egypte du crépuscule*, Chap. I: L'architecture et son décor, by François Saumas. Paris: Gallimard, 1978-1980.

LURKER, Manfred, *The Gods and Symbols of Ancient Egypt*, Eng. trans. Barbara Cummings. London & New York: Thames & Hudson, 1980.

MONTET, Pierre, *Tanis, douze années de fouilles dans une capitale oubliée du Delta égyptien*, Paris: 1942.

PEMBERTON, Delia, *Ancient Egypt, Architectural Guides for Travellers* series. London: Penguin, 1992.

PIRENNE, Jacques, *Histoire de la civilisation de l'ancienne Egypte*, 3 vols. Neuchâtel: 1961-1963.

SAUNERON, Serge and STIERLIN, Henri, *Edfou et Philae, derniers temples d'Egypte*, Paris: 1975.

SAUNERON, Serge, *The Priest of Ancient Egypt*, New York: 1980.

STIERLIN, Henri, *Egypte, des origines à l'islam*, Paris: 1984.

STIERLIN, Henri, and ZIEGLER, Christiane, *Tanis trésors des pharaons*, preface by Jean Leclant. Paris: 1987.

VANDERSLEYDEN, Claude, ed., *Das alte Agypten, Propyläen Kunstgeschichte*, Berlin: 1975.

# MAP

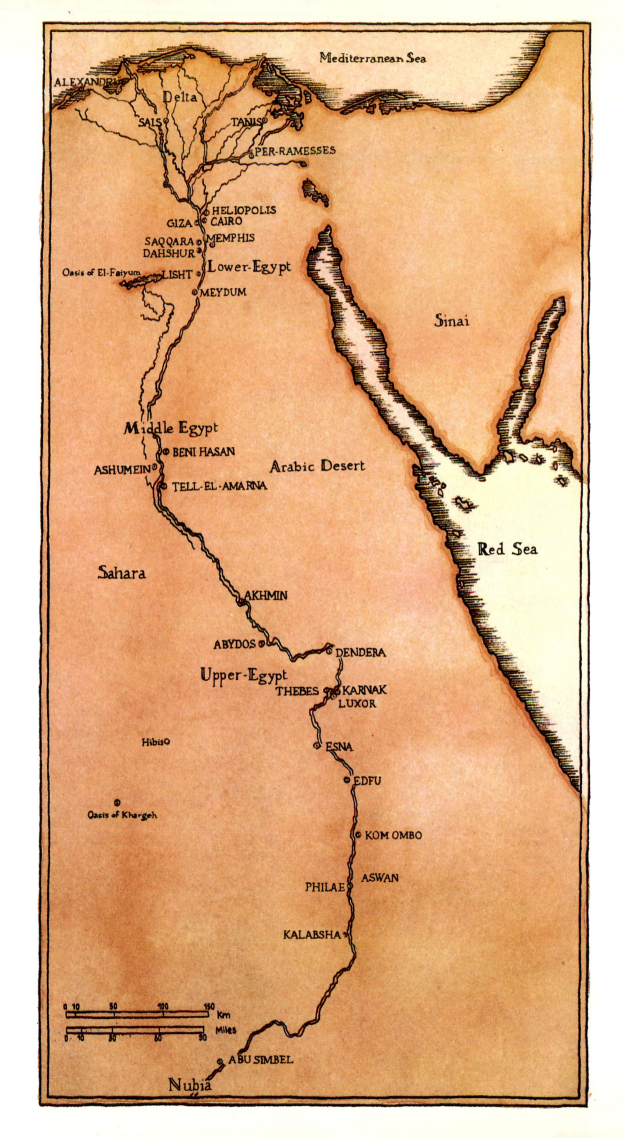

Mediterranean Sea

ALEXANDRIA

Delta

SAIS

TANIS

PER-RAMESSES

HELIOPOLIS

GIZA  CAIRO

SAQQARA  MEMPHIS

DAHSHUR

Oasis of El-Faiyum  LISHT  Lower-Egypt

MEYDUM

Sinai

Middle Egypt

BENI HASAN

ASHUMEIN

Arabic Desert

TELL-EL-AMARNA

Red Sea

Sahara

AKHMIN

ABYDOS

DENDERA

Upper-Egypt

THEBES  KARNAK

LUXOR

Hibis

ESNA

EDFU

Oasis of Khargeh

KOM OMBO

ASWAN

PHILAE

KALABSHA

0 10   50   100   150
Km

Miles
0 10   50   80   90

ABU SIMBEL

Nubia

# Index & Glossary

archi = architecture and archeology; art = artwork; Egypto = ancient Egyptian culture; fl = flourished around a date; k = king; loc = location; mytho = relating to gods; pl = plural; q = queen; numbers in bold refer to captions; all dates are BC unless otherwise indicated

# Chronology

| | |
|---|---|
| **PREHISTORY** Neolithic toward 5500 | Agriculture in the Valley of the Nile, first signs of artwork. |
| Chalcolithic 3500 | Nagada: copper smelting and pottery in Lower Egypt. |
| **PREDYNASTIC PERIOD** 3200 | Monarchy of Buto in Lower Egypt. |
| **FIRST DYNASTIES** 3000 | Menes unifies the Delta and Upper Egypt: capital Memphis. Thinite Period: 1st and 2nd Dynasties, of kings from Thinis, near Abydos. |
| 2800 | Djoser found Third Dynasty at Memphis. Imhotep, Djoser's architect: first pyramid at Saqqara. |
| **OLD KINGDOM** 2720 | Snoferu founds the Fourth Dynasty at Meydum, pyramid of Meydum and two pyramids of Dahshur. |
| 2690 | Kheops: great pyramid of Giza and royal barques. |
| 2660 | Khephren: second pyramid of Giza, great sphinx. |
| 2600 | Mykerinus: third pyramid of Giza. |
| 2560 | Userkaf founds the Fifth Dynasty. *Texts of the Pyramids.* |
| 2420 | Teti founds the Sixth Dynasty |
| 2330 | Reign of King Pepi II lasts more than ninety years. |
| **FIRST INTERMEDIATE PERIOD** 2240 | Revolution and upheavals throughout Egypt |
| 2200 | Pillage of the pyramids and tombs of the Old Kingdom Seventh and Tenth Dynasties at Memphis. |
| **MIDDLE KINGDOM** 2050 | Reunification and restoration by Mentuhotep I who founds Eleventh Dynasty: capital at Thebes in Upper Egypt. Funerary temple of Deir el-Bahri. |
| 2000 | Twelfth Dynasty: capital Lisht in Lower Egypt |
| 1970 | Sesostris I, White Chapel of Karnak. |
| 1785 | End of the Twelfth Dynasty. |
| **SECOND INTERMEDIATE PERIOD** 1780 | Thirteenth and Fourteenth Dynasties: disorders Hyksos invaders penetrate into the Delta. |
| 1680 | Fifteenth and Sixteenth Dynasties of Hyksos rulers Occupation of Egypt, capital Avaris in the Delta |
| 1600 | Independent kingdom at Thebes. Seventeenth Dynasty. Kamosis reconquers Middle Egypt. |
| **NEW EMPIRE** 1580 | Ahmose expels the Hyksos and founds the Eighteenth Dynasty Capital in Thebes in Upper Egypt. |
| 1560 | Amenophis I. |
| 1530 | Tuthmosis I. |
| 1520 | Tuthmosis II. |
| 1500 | Reign of Queen Hatshepsut with her vizier Senenmut. Temple of Hatshepsut at Deir el-Bahri. Tuthmosis III ascends the throne |
| 1483 | Tomb in the Valley of the Kings. |
| 1450 | Amenophis II. |

| | |
|---|---|
| 1408 | Amenophis III: colossi of Memnon; temple built by royal architect Amenotep-son-of-Hapu; temple of Karnak. |
| 1372 | Amenophis IV, the heretic pharaoh who calls himself Akhenaten. Religious crisis. Founds the city of Akhetaten in Tell el-Amarna in Middle Egypt. |
| 1354 | Tutankhaten becomes Tutankhamun; capital returns to Thebes. |
| 1343 | Reign of King Horemheb. Start of the great hypostyle hall of the Temple of Amun of Karnak. |
| 1314 | Ramesses I founds the Nineteenth Dynasty reigning with his son Sethos I. Osireion temple of Abydos. Additions to Temple of Amun at Karnak. |
| 1301 | Ramesses II founds new capital of Per-Ramesses in Delta : Thebes remains religious capital. Completion of hypostyle hall of Temple of Amun at Karnak construction of speos of Abu Simbel and of Ramesseum at Thebes. Tomb of Ramesses II in the Valley of the Kings and end of his 66-year reign. |
| 1235 | Dynastic crisis under King Merenptah. |
| 1219 | Reigns of Sethos II and Siptah. |
| 1205 | Period of disorder: invasions of Libyans and Peoples of the Sea are crushed. Syrian Kings ascend the throne. |
| 1200 | Expulsion of foreigners, founding of Twentieth Dynasty. |
| 1198 | Reign of Ramesses III: restoration and unification of Egypt. Construction of the Medinet Habu temple. |
| 1168 | Decline of the Ramesside kings from the Ramesses IV to IX. High priest Herihor assumes rule of Upper Egypt. |
| **THIRD INTERMEDIATE PERIOD** 1085 | Smendes founds Twenty-First Dynasty at Tanis in the Delta. |
| 1054 | Psusennes I reigns from Tanis. |
| 950 | Shoshenq founds the Twenty-Second "Libyan" Dynasty in Tanis. |
| toward 925 | Shoshenq takes Jerusalem and plunders the temple of Solomon. |
| 925 | Reign of Osorkon I. |
| 800 | Rise to power of the Nubians. |
| **KUSHITE, SAITE AND PERSIAN PERIODS** 715 | Nubian and Kushite Empires with capitals at Meroe and Napata. |
| 667 | Assurbanipal takes Thebes. |
| 663 | Psammetichus founds the Twenty-Sixth Dynasty: Saite renaissance. |
| 525 | Egypt conquered by a Persian ruler, Cambyses. |
| 378 | Nectanebo I founds the Thirtieth Dynasty. |
| 341 | Antaxerxes III plunders Egypt. |
| **PTOLEMAIC PERIOD** 332 | Alexander the Great at Memphis. |
| 331 | Foundation of the city of Alexandria. |
| 304 | Lagide Dynasty: reign of Ptolemy Soter at Alexandria. |
| 237 | Start of the temple of Edfu. |
| 80 | Start of the temple of Dendera. |
| BC 30 | End of the Ptolemy lineage. |
| **EGYPT A ROMAN PROVINCE** AD 37 | First hypostyle hall of Dendera |
| 41 | Hypostyle hall of Esna. |
| 117 | Kiosk of Trajan at Philae. |
| 395 | Last hieroglyphs at Philae. |
| 470 | Last texts in demotic. |
| 550 | Closing of the temple of Isis at Philae. |

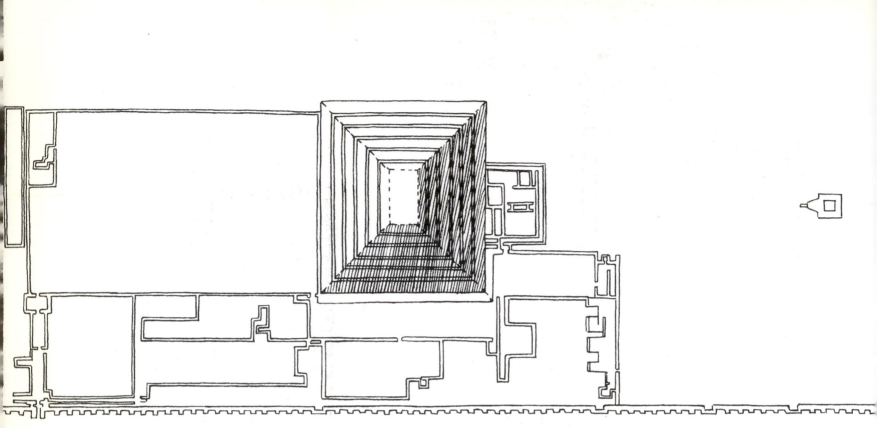

1. Plan of the funerary complex of Djoser at Saqqara.

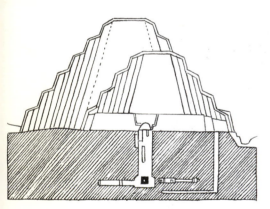

2. Cross section of Pyramid of Djoser.

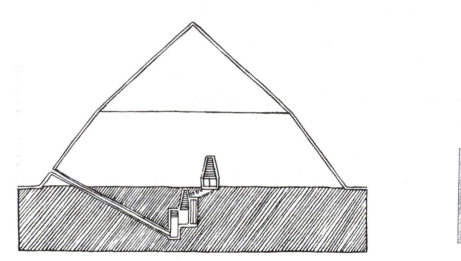

3. Cross section of Bent Pyramid of Snefru at Dashur.

5. Cross section of the Great Pyramid
   of Kheops at Giza.

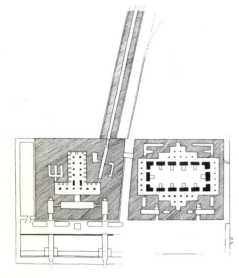

4. Plan of the Valley Temple of Khephren
   and Temple of the Sphinx at Giza.

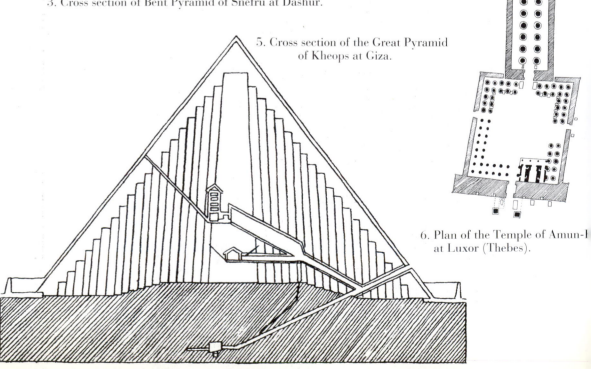

6. Plan of the Temple of Amun-R
   at Luxor (Thebes).

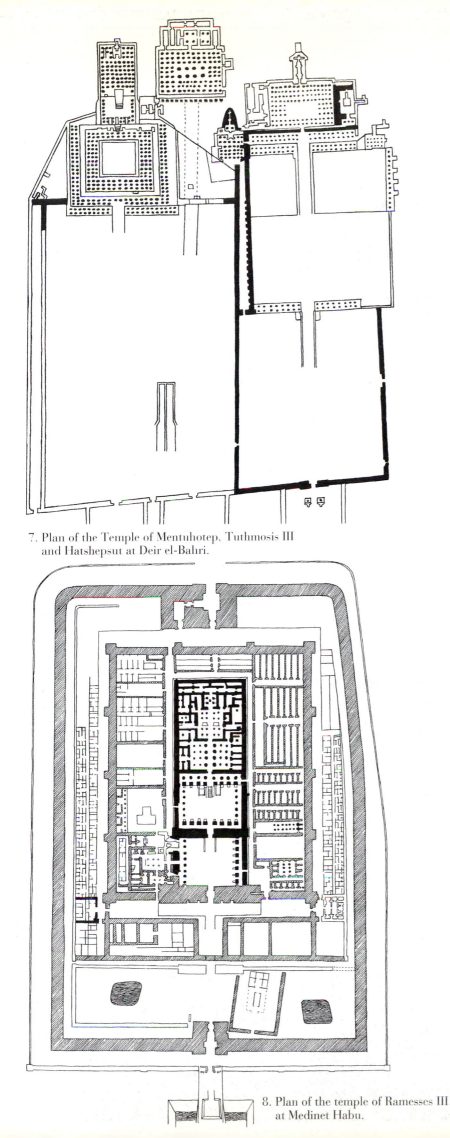

7. Plan of the Temple of Mentuhotep. Tuthmosis III
and Hatshepsut at Deir el-Bahri.

8. Plan of the temple of Ramesses III
at Medinet Habu.

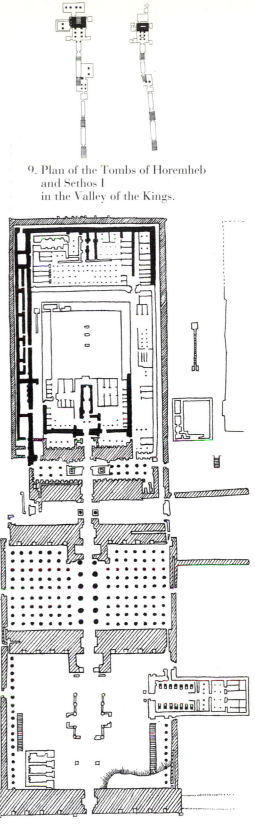

9. Plan of the Tombs of Horemheb
and Sethos I
in the Valley of the Kings.

10. Plan of the Great Temple of Amun at Karnak.

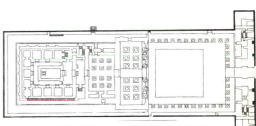

11. Plan of the Temple of Horus at Edfu.

1/2500

0 5 10  20        50              100        M

0 10 20  50      100           200          300  F T

**Statue of the celebrated architect Amenhotep-son-of-Hapu, seated as a scribe.**
(Egyptian Museum, Cairo)

# Acknowledgments

The author and publishers would like to take this opportunity to thank the following authorities which have allowed these photographs to be taken at sites as well as inside museums:

Department of Antiquities, Cairo

Cairo Museum

Museum of Ancient Egyptian Art, Luxor

Le département d'Egyptologie du Musée du Louvre, Paris,

The directors of the Museo Egizio, Turin

For the reproduction of historical documents, they express their gratitude to:

la direction de la Bibliothèque publique et universitaire and the Bibliothèque de la Grange, Geneva.

The Antikenmuseum in Basel and the séminaire d'egyptologie of the University of Basel.

For the two photographs published on pages 16 and 17, authorized by the Egyptian Department of the British Museum in London and by Franck Teichmann of Stuttgart.

All the other photographic documents were made by Anne and Henri Stierlin during visits to Egypt, the principal museums of Egyptology and many libraries.

Printed in Italy
La Zincografica Fiorentina